Running by
THE BOOK

BECOMING PHYSICALLY AND SPIRITUALLY FIT

CORINNE BAUR

BP
RESOURCES
PUBLISHINGYOURWORK.COM

PublishingYourWork
Berea, Kentucky
publishingyourwork.com

Editing, layout, and composition by PublishingYourWork.com.
Cover design by Convertible Creative.

ISBN 978-1-46367032-0

Printed in the United States of America

What others are saying about Running by The Book:

"*Running by The Book is a must-read for those who want to take their running and their spiritual life to a whole new level! This book uniquely combines a training program for a half marathon with a guide to growing closer to God in the process. It's a program that just makes sense.*"

Jean Blackmer, author of *MomSense: A Common-Sense Guide to Confident Mothering*

"*This book offers a dual approach to healthier living. If you read it and apply the advice provided, you too can achieve higher levels of spiritual and physical fitness. Let Christ come alongside, and lead while you run, then you can realize the best of both goals.*"

Tony Whitney, founder of Health Fitness Ministries

"*I am really excited about this book and look forward to recommending it to new and experienced runners alike. Having completed multiple half marathons and marathons I am familiar with the ups and downs of the life of an amateur runner—the challenge of trying to fit training into a busy schedule, the importance of a good training plan, the benefits of being a part of a running community, and the multiple spiritual principles and images that can be directly applied and more clearly understood through the training and race day experiences. I am adding this book to my list of needs for beginning runners: proper shoes, shorts, a watch, and 'Running by The Book.'*"

Jeremy Thiessen, drummer for the band Downhere—recipients of 2007–2009 Juno Award for Best Contemporary Christian/Gospel Album

"*Corinne Baur has such a unique concept. I'm not a runner, but I love her ability to weave running concepts and scripture together.*"

Nathan Whitaker, co-author of New York Times best sellers *Quiet Strength* with Tony Dungy, *Uncommon, The Mentor Leader,* and most recently *Through My Eyes* with Tim Tebow.

"*As a leader in search of Bible studies that I can recommend to women, I was excited to read Corinne's book that challenged both the spiritual life and the physical. Running a half marathon always seemed an impossible dream for me and so I couldn't wait to start the 12 weeks of training to challenge myself. I was encouraged, stretched, and inspired by the women who joined our team. I have now finished my first half marathon and am ready to dream bigger dreams!*"

Christy Hires, Director of Women to Women, Calvary Bible Church, Boulder, Colorado

"*I love how Corinne has helped me connect my physical condition to my spiritual life. As a pastor for 30 years, I have always known at some level that the two were connected. However, as Corinne challenged me to begin running seriously, she helped me to see so many specific connections between my spiritual race and the physical one. The daily disciplines, the necessity of building rest and recovery into the routine, the perseverance, the encouragement, the celebration of victories, and the picking back up after falling down… these and so many more lessons have been reinforced by my running training. They help me daily as I apply the lessons learned to my spiritual journey. I am so blessed that Corinne has encouraged me to run this race and has coached me so well.*"

Max Wilkins, Senior Pastor, The Family Church, Gainesville, Florida

My Lord, Jesus, you are the reason I wrote this book. Thank you for saving me. I humbly pray that your Kingdom is glorified through my life.

Running by The Book Communities

Christian running coach Corinne Baur is passionate about helping churches and groups create faith-based running programs. To help group leaders, Corinne has compiled a RBTB Leader's guide, offering chapter by chapter suggestions, tips and solutions for leading a successful Running by The Book group, available for free at RunningByTheBook.com.

Visit her Facebook site at facebook.com/RunningByTheBook where you can join her online community for tips, encouragement and meet others on their "race."

If you are interested in having Corinne speak to your group, please contact her at: info@runningbythebook.com.

Acknowledgments

There are so many people who have encouraged me throughout the journey of writing this book that if I thanked everyone personally it would be a book by itself! So thank you to all of my family and friends who have encouraged, read, prayed, given suggestions, and pointed out my mistakes along the way. You know who you are and I am so grateful to each of you!

Weston, you not only supported me one hundred percent, but bought me my own computer, did the dishes, cleaned the house, folded the laundry, picked the kids up from school and made me pots and pots of coffee so I could meet my deadlines and stay focused on my writing. Besides being the best friend and husband I could ever ask for, you are the perfect business manager! I feel protected and safe, knowing you are watching out for me. I praise God for choosing you for me, and I could not have finished this project without you.

To my wonderful children: you sweetly asked me every day if I had a good day of writing and waited patiently for me to finish my thoughts before asking if you could borrow my computer! I love you and am so very proud of who you are. You are my treasures and I am blessed to be your mother.

Kelly Shore, you are my spiritual mentor. Thank you for being obedient to the Lord. You love me unconditionally, know exactly when to call me, have just the right words to lift my spirits and are not afraid to tell me the truth—even when I don't really want to hear it. Thank you for believing in me all these years.

To my first running and walking groups: thank you so much for the inspiration! I am humbled by your determination and perseverance.

To my editor, Brian, you knew when to push me and when to let me relax. Your words of encouragement always came exactly when I needed them. I may not have made every deadline, but knowing I had someone holding me accountable truly helped me stay on track. Thank you for believing in my vision and making it a reality.

Thanks also to my awesome marketing team, who saw something worthwhile in this project. I am excited to team up with such talent!

Contents

Introduction

Congratulations! You're about to embark on a great adventure that will transform your self-image, your relationship with God—and your life! Whether you are a seasoned or recreational runner, feel solid in your Christian faith or have just begun down your Christian path, my prayer is that this experience will encourage you physically and spiritually, and awaken a deep desire for God in your life.

I do not pretend to be a great writer or a deep theologian; nor am I a star athlete. I have weaknesses, failings, and baggage, just like you. I come to you with only the experience that God has given me, doing my best to be obedient to His will. What you are holding in your hands is a part of my journey—one I hope you will relate to as a fellow Christian on your own journey. I am excited to share this part of our journeys together!

Growing up, I was one of the last ones picked for teams in gym class. In elementary school, because of my small stature, I was pulled out of afternoon recess once a week to join a gym class that today would be called "ESE." I never played a team sport, and never considered myself athletic. As I got older, I knew I should exercise, but life seemed to get in the way.

Drawn in by a good cause

In 2005, a friend and I decided to walk a half marathon as a fundraiser for a charity organization. I figured it was for a good cause, and—with three small children at home and a fairly large family business that I ran with my husband—the training would give me some much needed "me" time; plus it would force me to exercise! We were teamed up with a coach and given a training plan. About halfway into it, we realized we were capable of walking a full marathon. By the time we finished training, we were able to run the entire race.

I loved what the training did for me! I had more energy during the day and slept better at night. My clothes fit better, and I felt strong. I loved the camaraderie of training with a group of people who were working toward the same goal.

I didn't want that to go away, so I signed up for another half marathon. Half marathons are my personal favorite, by the way, because the distance requires diligent training, but is not as time consuming as a full marathon. Half marathons are a distance I never grow tired of. Each one brings new goals, experiences, and lessons! Because I no longer had my group to train with, I found running alone gave me time to pray, listen to praise music, and worship God. I started looking forward to training—not just for its own sake, but because I was getting closer to God!

Since then, I've advanced to running a 50K in the mountains, earned my Road Runners Club of America long-distance running coach certification, and become a certified National Academy of Sports Medicine Personal Trainer. I have coached beginners through their first race and seasoned runners to a better finish time. I devour books on nutrition and fitness.

All this from an undersized girl who was the last person anyone would have considered athletic. And you know what? I'm still not the fastest or most athletic out there. I'll probably never win a race, but I'm healthier, more energetic, more confident, and closer to God than I have ever been. If I can do it, I'm positive that you can, too.

Over the next 12 weeks, we will:
- engage in a running training program five days a week;
- uncover the relationship between our physical body and our spiritual journey;
- become fitter physically, as well as spiritually;
- pursue God in all that we do;
- finish with a formal half-marathon race; and
- recover and plan for the future.

I am so excited that you have decided to embark on this amazing journey in pursuit of a loving, powerful God who wants nothing more than to spend time with you! This program is unlike any training program or Bible study you have ever participated in. Not just an endurance training program and not just a Bible study, we will spend the next twelve weeks getting closer to God by strengthening our physical bodies, minds, and spirits. My prayer is that through this training you will find that you hunger for His presence, and you will feel a deeper, more satisfying sense of closeness to Him than ever before.

Before we lace up our running shoes and head out the door, let's discuss a minimum fitness level to get started. This training program assumes you can comfortably run 3–4 miles at a time, 3–4 days per week. *[Update: See the Author's PostScript at the end of this introduction for new information on how beginners can use this training to prepare for a 10K in 12 weeks!]* Why? In order to safely train for a half marathon in twelve weeks, you have to have a little bit of a running base to start with. A person with no training and no base can certainly progress up to a half marathon, but it takes longer than twelve weeks. So if you are unable to comfortably run 3–4 miles, 3–4 times per week right now, I highly suggest that you take several weeks to build up to this base. If you jump right in to this training program without that minimum base, you may become injured.

Don't be discouraged if you aren't there yet—I started at zero miles, zero days a week, a few years ago myself. All it took was a little bit of commitment and following a training program, and even I—an unfit, exhausted, working mom of three—was able to work up to half marathon training and beyond! I look forward to seeing you back here in a few weeks, ready to go!

Safety first!

Appendix A contains a Physical Activity Readiness Questionnaire (PAR-Q). I want you to fill it out—completely honestly—before you begin. Although it is safe for most people to be physically active, some people should check with their doctor before increasing their level of activity. If you answer yes to any of the questions, get permission from your doctor before beginning this training program.

Now that we have established that you have passed the minimum mileage base and have passed the PAR-Q, let's dive into what this training program is all about. You can certainly do it by yourself, but I hope you have (or will find) a group to train with. I recommend getting together twice a week for one mid-week run and one weekend long run. You can discuss one of the study day discussions after each run or do both after one of them.

Twice a week may seem like a bit much; I know that most people are used to group Bible studies that meet only once a week. But remember, this program isn't your typical Bible study. Meeting for a run twice a week helps to ensure that you are progressing in the training program and will be able to successfully run a half marathon. Knowing there are other people waiting for you will hold you accountable for your training that day—especially on those days you'd rather stay in bed! And there is no better way to end a long run than with a cup of coffee and a bagel with a group of running buddies. So grab a couple of friends and commit to training and learning together.

Equipment—simple, but critical

I am sure you are raring to go, but before you can head out the door for your first training run, we need to discuss running gear and running pace. Yes, I know you are already actively running, but we're about to increase your distance and time spent on the road…so getting the basics down properly is even more important.

Good running shoes are the single most important piece of equipment a runner can have. Running shoes can make or break your training. Running in worn-out shoes or shoes that are not right for your feet can lead to a painful run, at the least, and serious injury, at the worst. If you have never been fitted for running shoes, I highly recommend that you go to your local specialty running store for a professional fitting.

Even if you have been fitted in the past, if it has been over a year, I recommend that you get fitted again. Fluctuations in your weight, pregnancies, past injuries, and even age can change our feet, requiring a different shoe than you used in the past. A quality running store will analyze your gait, determining the best trade-off of cushion versus stability. Expect to spend a least $100 for a good pair of running shoes. Anything less will not last as long. When it comes to running shoes, you do get what you pay for.

But what about...

…the barefoot running craze? Would you be better off to train with no shoes? That's a heated topic in the running world. In my roles as long-distance running coach and certified trainer, I have talked with numerous doctors and physical therapists about this. My conclusion is that while barefoot running *may* have its place in training for some people, I can't recommend that the average runner run barefoot regularly. The research that seems to indicate that we were made to run without shoes doesn't take into account that the average American is mostly sedentary and has spent a majority of his or her life wearing shoes!

It's true that you will strengthen your feet—and possibly even improve your running form—if you run without shoes *on a soft, grassy surface* for a small amount of time. However, I personally believe that if an average person ran without shoes for miles on pavement, muscular injury would most likely occur. I don't think we will know the true benefits or repercussions of barefoot running for several years. So while I'm not saying *never* run barefoot, I am saying that it is in your best interest to get a good pair of running shoes that are right for your feet and running gait.

While you are buying shoes, buy a quality pair of running socks. A quality running sock is made of "technical material" (which means no cotton) that wicks the moisture from your foot so it can dissipate out your shoe. Cotton socks hold moisture, keeping your feet moist; and moist feet are prone to blisters. A dry foot is a happy foot. There are many different types of running socks, from micro-thin, low-cut ankle socks to super-cushioned crew socks. What brand and type is your personal choice; just be sure the sock is cotton-free.

Women, a quality running bra will increase your running enjoyment and comfort tremendously. Look for a bra that is made for "high-impact" sports. The rule of thumb is to buy a new running bra with every pair of shoes, or when the tag on the bra becomes unreadable. This is especially true for larger sizes. The straps stretch as they age and don't offer the right support. Replacing them this often may seem a bit excessive, but in the long run, you will be glad you did.

> *Your running socks and technical running clothes won't wick moisture away if you wash them with fabric softener. The fabric softener clogs the material's pores. If you forget and use softener, don't worry— just wash them again,—the softener will rinse out, and they will be good as new!*

While I consider quality running shoes, socks, and a high-impact sports bra necessities, the rest of your gear is more flexible. I do recommend technical running clothes. Anything that touches your body should be made of wicking material. Again, cotton holds moisture and can make for an uncomfortable run. These days, you can find decent, but inexpensive running clothes, even in discount stores.

You may want to purchase a stopwatch. It can be as simple as a single-function stopwatch or as technical as a GPS watch/heart rate monitor. It depends on how much money you want to spend; and you can start simple and improve your tools as you improve your skills, but you will find that at least having a stopwatch will be helpful in tracking your time.

In week six, we'll talk about your heart rate and how tracking it can help in your training, so you may want to consider a watch that includes a heart rate chest strap and monitor. It's not necessary, but can be helpful.

Don't just start running

So now we're well dressed, but still not quite ready to start running. In Appendix B you'll find more information on warming up and cooling down. This explains dynamic stretches versus static stretches and how to do them. You will do dynamic stretches before you run, and static stretches after you run. Each run should also consist of a 5- to 10-minute warm-up and cool-down period. Start by walking, and slowly increase your pace until you are at your training speed. The key is to gradually warm up your muscles, getting oxygen flowing through them, and slowly raising your heart rate. The last 5-10 minutes of your run should be spent slowing your pace until you are walking and your heart rate and breathing are no longer elevated.

Your training pace (the speed that you run at in between the warm-up and cool-down) should be a nice, slow, easy pace. These should not be sprints or time trials. During your run, you should be able to pass the "talk test," meaning you should be able to speak in complete sentences. If you have to take a breath between words, you need to slow down. If I am running by myself, I like to sing out loud for a few minutes to make sure I am not breathing too heavily. I may sound strange to those passing by, but at least I am not running too fast!

The biggest mistake people make when beginning a training program is starting out too fast. If you find that you need to take a break or two to slow to a walk, go ahead. Again, we are looking for endurance, not speed; so there is nothing wrong with walking for a few minutes during your run. In fact, if a run/walk program appeals to you, turn to Appendix F for tips on how to effectively incorporate walking into your training.

Using this training plan

Now, let's go over how to use this book. There are twelve weeks of physical training with twelve weeks of corresponding Bible study. At the beginning of each chapter, you will find each week's training schedule. I encourage you to cut out each schedule and hang it on your refrigerator, or wherever it will remind you to train. You can also download and print out all training schedules from my Web site, Run-ningByTheBook.com.

Each weekly schedule includes 4 days of running, 1 day of cross-training, and 2 rest days. Three of the runs on this schedule are measured by time without concern for dis-tance, and the last one is a specific distance—no matter how long it takes.

If life gets busy and you need to rearrange your workout days one week, no problem; but do your best to have a full week between long runs, or you'll be putting too much stress on your body.

The cross-training day (x-train) is a day to do another endurance activity for the amount of time listed, such as biking, swimming, or walking. Pick an activity that will get you moving, but will give your running muscles a rest. (Yes, walking uses different muscles). If you can't stand cross-training or do not have access to a bike or pool, it's OK to substitute another easy run on that day. I personally like cross-training because I can still raise my heart rate and train my cardiovascular system, but I give my running muscles a break.

The workout days are flexible, so you can choose which workout to do on what day, but it's best to be consistent each week with your long run. For instance, choose Saturday as your day to do long runs.

Finally, rest days are just that—days to rest from training. My favorite days to rest are right before and after my long run.

Underneath the weekly schedule, you will see a row of blank squares. This is your log, where you will write what you actually did that day, along with a couple of words that describe how the workout went. For example, if your schedule stated "Easy run 30 min.," but you only ran for 25 minutes because your calf cramped and you had to quit, you would write something like "ran 25, left calf cramped." If you had a great run, write something about why it was so great ("beautiful day," "praise music moved me," and so on).

Following the training schedule is the weekly Bible study, broken up into two days of homework. This is where we will explore the relationship between training for a half marathon and the path we are walking with God. It is my prayer that a physical training program coupled with biblical exploration of the parallels between our physical bodies and our spiritual walk will lead you to love God more and desire to pursue Him with all of your heart. God has a race for each of us, if we choose to follow Him. May this program encourage you to "run the race God has set before [you]" (Hebrews 12:1).

Each day of homework will find us in God's Word, looking up Scripture, and applying it to our lives. The questions will be discussed in your group. If you don't feel like sharing a particular answer, that's OK; but I find that I learn so much from those who choose to share their thoughts with the group.

I look forward to meeting you on the pages of your first week! Run safe! And remember, *easy* pace!

Author's PostScript

When I first wrote this book, I intended it for those who wanted to train for a half marathon. I have discovered through my pilot programs that there are usually a handful of people who want to participate in the program and training but are not quite ready, physically or mentally, to jump into half marathon mileage. Instead, they have opted to alter the training plan mileage, especially the weekly long run, and train for a 10K (6.2 miles).

A healthy, injury-free person who has little to no running experience really can train for a 10K in twelve weeks! So I have added Appendix G containing a 10K training program. If you are not prepared to begin a half marathon program, then this 10K program is for you! When I mention that you need to be able to comfortably run 3–4 miles at a time, 3–4 days per week in the introduction, that is a running base needed to safely train for a half marathon, not a 10K. Again, a healthy, injury-free person should be able to train for a 10K in 12 weeks, even with no previous experience.

If you are starting from zero miles, make it your goal to walk a 10K at the end of twelve weeks. Wherever I mention "running", substitute "walking." Whenever I mention specific half marathon mileage like 13.1 miles, substitute your 10K mileage of 6.2 miles. The truths in this study work for both a 10K and half marathon, and you should be proud of any mileage you accomplish.

Sign up for a 10K now! Many half marathons have 10K races the same weekend. And I challenge you: once you successfully complete your 10K, don't quit! You now have the base needed to begin training for a half marathon!

Week 1

God's Training Plan

After completing this week's training and homework, you will be able to:

- understand the benefits of using a training plan to train for a half marathon,
- see the Bible as our spiritual training plan,
- define "specificity in training," and
- see the benefits of filling out a training log and spiritual journal.

Study Day One

But even more blessed are all who hear the word of God and put it into practice.
Luke 11:28

Today starts a journey of physical and spiritual growth. I am so excited to be on this journey with you, and am very proud of you for making the commitment to train for a half marathon while strengthening your relationship with God. I am continually amazed at what He reveals to me while I am running, and my prayer is that you, too, will find Him on the roads and trails that make up your training.

If you haven't already signed up for a half marathon, I encourage you to go to RunningByTheBook.com and follow the links to various races around the country. It may seem premature to sign up for a half marathon already—the idea of running 13.1 miles may seem impossible right now—but signing up for a race will give you accountability to complete your training. I don't know about you, but I sometimes need a deadline to get me to actually complete my goal!

If your race registration requires an estimated finish time, it is best to estimate on the slow side. Finishing a half marathon in 2 hours requires running 9 minutes per mile, 2.5 hours is about 11.5 minutes per miles, and 3 hours is close to 14 minutes per mile. Do your best to figure out where you fall within these times, and err on the slow side.

Sign up for a half marathon that falls as close to the end of these twelve weeks as possible. You really do need twelve weeks to train, so don't sign up for one that is closer than twelve weeks out. If you choose to sign up for a race that is further out, you can repeat our training plan for weeks 10 and 11 until race week. Participating in a half marathon race will be the perfect celebration for all of the hard work, spiritually and physically, that you will have accomplished at the end of our time together. So, before going any further, find a race and sign up!!

Stick with the plan

I get really excited when I start a new training plan! I love the anticipation of all of the challenges and accomplishments that lie ahead. I never know what my life will bring while I am training for a race, but at least I know what my training weeks will look like. Before we launch into it, though, I think it's important to spend a moment on why it's important to follow this training program rigorously.

Imagine that I saw an advertisement for a fun-looking half marathon coming up in a couple of months. The free T-shirt looks pretty good; and hey, I've always wanted to try to run a half marathon, so I decide to sign up.

Week 1 TRAINING SCHEDULE

There are 5 workouts (4 runs, 1 cross training) and 2 rest days each week.
The workout days are flexible, however use 1 rest day after your longest run.

WEEK 1	WORKOUT 1	WORKOUT 2	WORKOUT 3	WORKOUT 4	WORKOUT 5	WORKOUT 6	WORKOUT 7
PLAN	Easy Run 35 min	X-train 30 min	Easy Run 30 min	Easy Run 35 min	Rest	Long Run 5 miles	Rest
LOG							

Always spend 5-10 minutes warming up and 5-10 minutes cooling down. This can be included in your total time/mileage.

Long Run: These should be at an easy, conversational pace.
Easy Run: Easy runs should be at an easy, conversational pace. On a scale of 1-10 (10 being all out effort), an easy run should feel like a 5-6.
X-train: Cross-training. Anything other than running, such as swimming, biking, walking, strength training.
LOG: This is where you write what you ACTUALLY did that day, along with a description of how you prepared and how you felt.

"Blessed are all who hear the word of God and put it into practice." — LUKE 11:28

(This page is left blank so that you can cut out the workout plan on the other side and display it where you'll see it regularly.)

As the weeks roll by, I run a few miles here and there whenever I feel like it. Life gets in the way, and I find that days go by without running. One day, instead of running, I decide to go to a rock climbing gym; another day I give Zumba® a try. I never diligently follow a running plan that safely increases my miles each week.

You'll find that we do have cross-training time in our plan, so you can enjoy other activities while you train; but that doesn't mean you can substitute in those activities on running days.

Do you think I would successfully complete the half marathon? It's pretty unlikely. I would probably run part of it, feeling pretty good. Soon fatigue and pain would kick in as I pushed my muscles and cardiovascular system past what I had trained them to do. There would be serious risk of injury.

If my injury did not sideline me right away, eventually I would slow down and then stop before I reached the finish—exhausted, discouraged, every muscle aching. On the race results page, beside my name would be the dreaded DNF (Did Not Finish). I would be in severe pain for many days to follow, it would take a very long time to recover, and I may well give up running forever. I can't "try" to run 13.1 miles. I have to "train" to run 13.1 miles following a purposeful, focused plan.

As a certified, long-distance running coach with the Road Runners Club of America, I've seen all kinds of, well, *interesting* training plans thrown together; but a good training plan should be written by someone who has the experience and education to know how to start you where you are, and gradually and systematically progress you through various daily, weekly, and monthly goals so that at the end you are prepared for a successful race.

God has a training plan for you

I think wandering through our spiritual life without following a plan to continually strengthen our faith and relationship with God is just as foolish as

5

running a marathon without training! As John Ortberg says in his book, *The Life You've Always Wanted,* "There is an immense difference between training to do something and trying to do something. This need for training is not confined only to athletics...Indeed it is required for any significant challenge in life—including spiritual growth."[1]

Did you ever stop to think that God has an **awesome** training plan for us in His Word? The truths and promises found in His Word form the program we need to help us continually grow spiritually, and the encouragement of those who have gone before us provides hope that we, too, can finish our race strong.

Look up the following verses and write down what they reveal about God's Word:

2 Samuel 22:31 _____

_____

Proverbs 30:5 _____

_____

Hebrews 4:12 _____

_____

Isaiah 40:8 _____

_____

Luke 11:28 _____

_____

John 1:1 _____

_____

God is the ultimate coach! God's training plan for us is true, stands forever, and is full of power. We are blessed when we hear it and obey. My goal is that by the end of this twelve-week training program you will have the skills necessary to use His training program to strengthen and grow your spiritual training.

However great the training program, whether physical or spiritual, if you don't actually *do the training*, you won't be able to run a half marathon. You have to be committed to following the plan, as it is written.

Look back at our training schedule for this week. How many days this week will you devote to running? _____

How many days will you devote to cross-training (engaging in an activity that is not running, but is similar)? _____

Why do you think we are devoting so much time each week to running?

_____

_____

Specificity of training

An important principal of every training program is **specificity of training**. Simply put, in order to become proficient at running longer distances, we have to *specifically* practice running. If we don't spend most of our twelve weeks together running, we may become reasonably fit, but we will not be able to complete a half marathon. While swimming, Zumba, Pilates, and rock climbing are all physically beneficial activities, they will not train you to run 13.1 miles.

Is there a physical activity that you think you will need to give up for twelve weeks in order to more successfully train your half marathon race? If so, what is it?

_____

_____

Sometimes I think we need to put the principal of specificity of training in our spiritual lives as well! We can't attend every activity at church, make dinners for every potluck, and become so busy for His Kingdom that we neglect to spend time in His Word and in His presence. Beth Moore calls this "the captivity of activity."[2] She says there are times we need to focus our efforts so we have the energy to do what He has called us to do, and do it well.

The biblical story that always comes to my mind as I think about how I allow myself to become "busy for God" is when Jesus visits Mary and Martha in Luke 10:38-42. Take a moment to read the story now. How does Jesus respond when Martha asks Jesus to tell Mary to help in the kitchen?

_____

_____

Notice that Jesus isn't saying that preparing dinner is a bad thing; only that Mary's choice of spending time at His feet was the better choice in this instance. God wants us to take the time to get to know Him through His Word and to focus on those areas that will fulfill His purpose for us.

Before I began running, coaching, and writing, I enjoyed spending time making jewelry—especially bracelets with spiritual themes. I even sold them at local art shows. As God began to reveal His purpose for me through running, I put away my beads and wire because I realized that as much as I enjoy making jewelry and using my designs for God's Kingdom, it's a distraction from what God has purposed for me at this time. I still love making jewelry; and maybe, in time, I will get my beads back out, but until then, I am satisfied to give it up for God's greater purpose in my life.

Are you one of those with a tendency to try to do it all? _____

_____

If you answered yes, write a prayer asking God to help you determine what activities you may need to give up for a season so that you can spend time with Him, allowing Him to reveal what it is He has planned for you.

The bottom line is that without having a training program, we won't have the skills needed to help us successfully cross the finish line. Once we have a training plan, we have to be committed to following it, and possibly give up those things that keep us from being able to focus on our training.

During your next training run, spend some time meditating on where you spend your time with God. Are you scurrying around making meals, or are you spending time at His feet? Ask Him to reveal where *He* wants you to spend your time… and then listen.

Study Day Two

Every part of Scripture is God-breathed and useful one way or another—show-ing us truth, exposing our rebellion, correcting our mistakes, training us to live God's way. Through the Word we are put together and shaped up for the tasks God has for us.
2 Timothy 3:16-17 (Msg)

Hopefully you have had an opportunity to complete at least one day of training before beginning today's contemplation time. What was the hardest part about getting out to complete your training?

_____

_____

What aspect of running did you find most challenging? (pace, breathing, finishing the run...)

_____

_____

Don't be surprised if suddenly life starts getting in the way of your training. Although it is important to complete the training, Tim Noakes, MD and author of *The Lore of Running* says, "Don't set your daily training schedule in stone."[3] This is why you have five days of training and seven days to accomplish it. Remain flexible and positive so that no matter what life brings, you will still find the time to train.

If something really gets in the way (you get the stomach flu, or your child gets the stomach flu and you get no sleep), don't try to make up missed training by adding time or mileage onto another day. Consider your missed training a much-needed rest day and continue the training as written.

Don't forget that right now we are not worrying about speed. Your pace should be comfortable and easy. Remember that you should be able to speak in complete sentences while running. If you had to stop and walk in order to complete a sentence, that's fine. The point is to be on your feet for the amount of time listed on your training log, whether that time is spent walking or running.

If you finished your training and felt great—wonderful! *Resist the urge to run a few more minutes.* I'll talk more about why it's important to stick to the training schedule in Week 2.

In our last study session, we talked about the importance of a training plan, both for our physical growth and our spiritual growth. God's Word is our spiritual training plan.

How does Paul describe our training plan in the NLT translation of 2 Timothy 3:16-17? "All Scripture is inspired by _____ and is useful to teach us what is true and to make us realize what is wrong in our lives. It _____ and teaches us to do what is right. God uses it to _____ and _____ his people to do every good work."

We discussed specificity in training earlier. Thinking in both physical and spiritual terms, write the definition of "specificity in training" in your own words, without looking back at Day 1:

_____

_____

During your run this week, did you feel God reveal an activity that you may need to give up in order to spend more time with Him?

_____

_____

Your training log isn't optional

Today, we are going to discuss the importance of filling out a training log. As I explained in the introduction, a training log is where you write what you *actually* did versus what the plan says you should have done that day. Why is this important to document? Because life gets in the way! You get sick; you have an unexpected deadline at work; you go on vacation. I realize you probably won't complete every day of training exactly as it is written. (A good training program takes that into account!) But if you don't keep track of your progress, you won't have a true picture of how your training is actually going, and if anything needs to be tweaked.

Having an accurate picture of progression is important for several reasons. If you haven't completed a majority of the training for the week, it's probably not wise to jump right into the next week's training. Each week builds upon the training accomplished the week before. For instance, if I'm scheduled to run a total of 10 miles one week, but I only run 3 of them, I greatly increase my chance of injury if I try to tackle the 11 or 12 miles I am supposed to run the following week. The mileage jump is probably too big an increase for my body. Instead, I need to readdress my schedule for the next week, increasing my mileage based on how I actually trained.

Writing down a little about each run also helps you see patterns in your running. I do my best to write down what time of day I ran, where I ran, what I ate before and during, and how I felt during my run. If you notice that every time you run in the morning before breakfast you feel terrible, but you run great after you eat a piece of toast, you can assume that eating the toast helps you run better.

I know from my own training logs that I run better in the mornings after I have had a chance to pause and drink a cup of coffee with a piece of peanut butter toast. That doesn't mean I always get to run under those ideal conditions, but it gives me the knowledge that if I want to run really well, I should take the time to do the things that help me be my best.

You'll notice that I described a pre-run breakfast as coffee and peanut butter toast—not a doughnut. We'll talk more about nutrition later, but for now let me just say that how you fuel your body can make or break your run.

Again, the purpose of a training plan is to train us successfully to reach a goal. If we don't keep track of our progress, we won't know what specific things can help us reach that goal. The more detailed the training log, the easier it is to determine patterns that help and hurt.

But my favorite reason for keeping a detailed training log is for the encouragement. I love to be able to go back through my training logs and see how far I have come. This is especially helpful when I am going through a rough patch in my training. Sometimes just seeing where I came from, how many miles I have logged over the months, and how much faster I can now run the same distance is all the encouragement I need to get back out there and run another day.

Keeping a spiritual training log

God has given us His Word to train us to do what is right in His eyes and to show us where we have fallen short. Taking the time to reflect on whether we followed His plan or strayed off course allows us to see how much we need Christ in our lives. We can do that in prayer and in a journal. It helps to ask yourself questions about things that might be challenges in your life:

- Did I have patience with my kids today?
- Were my thoughts judgmental or compassionate?
- Am I shining Christ's love through my actions?
- Where did I rely on Him and allow Him to work through me?

We know that we will continually fail at His plan because we're sinners and fall short of the glory of God (Romans 3:23); but we can acknowledge where we failed, ask for forgiveness with a repentant heart, and do our best to follow His plan tomorrow—knowing that His grace will be there when we mess up again.

Have you ever kept a spiritual journal? _____

If the answer is yes, what prompted you to begin a spiritual journal and what about it encourages you the most?

_____

_____

_____

_____

If the answer is no, why not?

_____

_____

_____

_____

I know that a lot of people are uncomfortable with the idea of a spiritual journal. I certainly was for the longest time. I had absolutely no desire to write down what challenges I was going through, or put my prayer into written word. What if someone read it? I didn't even want to read what I might have written!

It wasn't until I began running and really feeling a closeness to God on my runs that I had any desire to begin a journal. At first, all I did was go to my Bible and look up and highlight passages of Scripture that had come to my mind while running. Then I began to write in the margins of my Bible the thoughts I had on those passages and why they were meaningful to me. Finally I began using a notebook. You're reading some of the fruit of those notebooks.

I'm not saying that you *must* keep a spiritual journal. After all, Jesus didn't. But I have found that copying down inspiring Scripture helps me stay focused on God's Word and what He wants for me. Instead of a million wandering thoughts interrupting the prayers that I say in my head, I find that praying on paper gives me focus and structure (and helps me stay awake—okay, I admit it, sometimes I fall asleep during prayer if I close my eyes and pray in my head). And if my prayers are too private to keep on paper, I tear them up in little pieces and throw them away! Jotting down a list of names helps me keep track of who is on my prayer list. Being actively involved in my quiet time and prayer time keeps my mind and spirit awake and aware of God's presence.

Through my journal I see how far I've grown, and areas where I seem to struggle repeatedly. Those can point to things that I still need to give to God. There are days that I go back through the thoughts I've written, and I can see God's hand all over my words. That makes Him feel more tangible and present in my life. Most encouraging to me, though, are the prayers I see He has answered—sometimes after a long time has gone by.

Remember, don't just read...do!

I encourage you to take a few minutes after your next run to jot down not only how far you ran and how you felt, but any thoughts that came to you that gave you a feeling of closeness to God.

I can't wait to see you on the pages of your study time next week. Starting anything new can be a challenge. I am proud of you for undertaking this training.

Building the Foundation through Core Training

After completing this week's training and homework you will be able to:

- define "base building,"
- see the significance of Jesus as our lives' base,
- engage your physical core, and
- list some spiritual core truths found in the Bible.

Study Day One

> *"He will be the sure foundation for your times,*
> *a rich store of salvation and wisdom and knowledge."*
> Isaiah 33:6 (NIV)

Congratulations on making it to your second week of training! I pray that you are beginning to find a routine that enables you to spend time each day training spiritually and physically.

Last week, we determined that in order to successfully train we first need a plan, and then we need to commit to following that plan. We also discussed using a training log to track our progress, see patterns in our training, and encourage us along the way. I hope you remembered to fill out your training log, and maybe even tried to maintain a spiritual journal in some way.

This week, we will spend time discussing building our training foundation and why this is so important. If you glance at this week's training schedule, you will note that we are still running at an easy, conversational pace, and our mileage/time is increasing just slightly from last week. The biggest increase is in our long run. The increases are slight because we are working on building a strong, solid foundation. This is called **base building** or endurance training. Building a strong foundation through gradual, gentle training is the first step to a great race.[1] Through this base-building phase, our bodies will make physical adaptations needed to run an endurance race, including:

- running muscles will learn to use available oxygen more efficiently,[2]
- improving ability to transport blood and oxygen to all muscles/organs,[3]
- strengthening connective tissue (joints, tendons, ligaments),[4]
- building stronger and more efficient cardiovascular and pulmonary systems,[5]
- learning to use fat as energy instead of carbohydrates,[6]
- increasing the number of capillaries in your muscles,[7]
- learning to tolerate moderate levels of lactic acid build-up in your muscles (lactic acid is a by-product of muscles that are oxygen depleted).[8]

There are no short cuts, no magic pills, no secret exercises we can do to quickly build our endurance base. These adaptations are made by slowly and methodically increasing our base mileage with easy training runs—where your pace allows you to breath smoothly enough to carry on a conversation. Running magazines and books are filled with story after story of people trying to short

Week 2 — TRAINING SCHEDULE

There are 5 workouts (4 runs, 1 cross training) and 2 rest days each week.
The workout days are flexible, however use 1 rest day after your longest run.

WEEK 2	WORKOUT 1	WORKOUT 2	WORKOUT 3	WORKOUT 4	WORKOUT 5	WORKOUT 6	WORKOUT 7
PLAN	Easy Run 35 min	X-train 30 min	Easy Run 30 min	Easy Run 40 min	Rest	Long Run 6 miles	Rest
LOG							

Always spend 5-10 minutes warming up and 5-10 minutes cooling down. This can be included in your total time/mileage.

Long Run: These should be at an easy, conversational pace.
Easy Run: Easy runs should be at an easy, conversational pace. On a scale of 1-10 (10 being all out effort), an easy run should feel like a 5-6.
X-train: Cross-training. Anything other than running, such as swimming, biking, walking, strength training.
LOG: This is where you write what you ACTUALLY did that day, along with a description of how you prepared and how you felt.

He will be the sure foundation for your times, a rich store of salvation and wisdom and knowledge. — ISAIAH 33:6 (NIV)

(This page was left blank so that you could cut out the workout plan on the other side and display it where you'll see it regularly.)

change this process and becoming injured. Shin splints, Achilles tendonitis, and plantar fasciitis are just a few of the common injuries that plague those who did too much, too soon.

Even if you feel your muscles are strong, resist the urge to run faster or farther than your plan. Tendons, joints and ligaments do not strengthen as quickly as muscle, so even though your muscles may be ready to go, your joints and tendons probably aren't.

Caution: If you begin to notice a nagging ache that is more than just a sore muscle, you may need to back off of your training a bit. Go to Appendix D and look up common running injuries and how to help them.

Another trap we can fall into is thinking we can cram all of our running into one or two days. I have trained people who (against my advice) only ran when our training group met. They figured that getting a long run in once or twice a week was as good as running consistently each day. When race day came, though, they didn't have the strong, solid base they needed to run their best. They felt miserable at the end of the race, and they didn't do nearly as well as they would have been capable of doing if they had spent the time to build a consistent, solid base.

Why is that so important? It's the day in, day out solid foundation that will give us the strength we need for harder workouts, such as longer distances, speed work, and hills. We can't safely increase our speed without a solid mileage base underneath our feet.

Base building is a phase that I return to over and over again in my training. As I plan my races and events each year, I make sure I allow myself plenty of time to build a solid base with gentle easy runs that gradually increase mileage over time. That ensures that I'll be able to run each race strong.

We need to have a good base in our spiritual walk as well. We need a strong, consistent foundation upon which we can build our faith. That foundation will hold us up during the tough times, and carry us through life's challenges. Look up Matthew 7:24 and Luke 6:47-49. Who is the foundation in these stories?

Even before Christ came to earth, Isaiah prophesied Christ as our foundation. In Isaiah 28:16, what words does the prophet use to describe Christ as our foundation?

It is on Christ, our precious cornerstone, that we must build our lives. Building our lives on anything other than Jesus will cause spiritual injury. In 1 Corinthians 3:11, Paul says, "No one can lay any other foundation than the one we already have—Jesus Christ." Jesus is our base; our strong foundation! The word foundation that Paul used here comes from the Greek word *themelios*, which can be translated "foundations, beginnings, first principals, of an institution or system of truth."[9] In other words, Jesus is our beginning, the foundation of our truth.

For me, recognizing that Christ is the firm foundation that I need to build my life upon has been a journey. It's not that I was purposely building on a weak foundation—I just didn't really give much thought to what I was basing life upon. Then when challenges came, I leaned on my own strength, my friends, things I read in books…anything but Christ. I just didn't know Him well enough to put my trust in His foundation.

The first step is recognizing intellectually that He is the only base strong enough to hold you up through everything life brings. Then, as you get to know Him, it gets easier and easier to trust Him with all your heart.

Do you find when you need a strong foundation that you find it in Christ or in something else?

_____

_____

My prayer is that you come to realize that Christ is the one and only foundation you need to build your life upon! According to Isaiah 33:6, what does the Lord provide us in as part of His "sure foundation"?

_____

_____

So Jesus offers His salvation, His wisdom, and His knowledge! But how do we access those things?

Jesus offers salvation.

Read the following verses, and write them in the spaces below:

Isaiah 12:2 _____

_____

John 3:16 _____

_____

John 3:36 _____

_____

Romans 10:9-10 _____

_____

Ephesians 2:8 _____

_____

Titus 3:5 _____

_____

When we accept the gift Jesus offers—believing that Jesus died on the cross for our sins, not because of anything we did, but because of His grace—we are given His gift of salvation. "If you confess with your mouth that Jesus is Lord and believe in your heart that God raised him from the dead, you will be saved" (Romans 10:9). This is the starting line of our spiritual journey, the beginning of our solid foundation in Christ.

I have to be honest here; at the moment I made the decision to follow Jesus, my life did not miraculously change. I know that some people have radical experiences, but it didn't happen that way for me. Nothing felt different. I did not suddenly have a burning desire to dig into the Bible or pray. It has been a slow, gradual process for me; a process through which, day by day, my relationship with Him grows and my foundation in Him strengthens as I purposely train in His ways.

As my foundation grows stronger in Him, my awe of His tremendous sacrifice and gift of salvation grows even greater. Nothing I did or can ever do will earn my salvation. It is a gift given to me because He loves me and wants to spend eternity with me. How awesome is that? It is a gift He offers to anyone who is willing to open their hearts to Him—even just a little—and trust that He died for all of us.

Perhaps you have never taken this step, but you feel God tugging at your heart. I encourage you to begin building that spiritual foundation right now. It's as simple as ABC:

"**A**"—Admit that you need a Savior. When Isaiah was taken into the presence of God, he realized immediately that he didn't measure up. His immediate response was: "It's all over! I am doomed, for I am a sinful man." (Isaiah 6:5). Just like Isaiah, we need to admit our sinfulness and our need for help.

"B"—Believe that the sacrifice Jesus made at the cross on our behalf did everything necessary for us to be forgiven. All that is necessary for us to receive that cleansing and forgiveness is to trust Jesus and believe that He died for our sins.

"C"—Confess Jesus as your Savior, both in your words and in your actions. We acknowledge to God that Jesus is our Savior, but also to other people. Paul says, "If you confess with your mouth that Jesus is Lord and believe in your heart that God raised him from the dead, you will be saved" (Romans 10:9).

That is our foundation of faith, and it is all that is needed to receive God's gracious gift of salvation. It is the first, most important step to take to building your foundation in Christ.

If you have already accepted Jesus as your Lord and Savior, I encourage you to reread those verses above and really meditate on them. I find it humbling and encouraging to continually return to God's plan of salvation. It reminds me that although I strive to follow His way, it is only through Christ's death and resurrection that I am saved.

Jesus offers knowledge and wisdom.

If salvation is the starting line of our spiritual walk, where do we go from there? Christ doesn't just want to save us ... He wants to join us on our journey, providing us with the knowledge and wisdom we need to successfully finish our race.

According to Colossians 2:2-4, what do we have in Christ?

_____

_____

_____

Remember last week when we discovered that God has a perfect training program for our spiritual walk? If you can, without looking, try to recall what we learned about His Word. (If you need a hint, go back to page 6.)

_____

_____

_____

_____

As we delve into God's training plan by spending time in His Word, we will have access to that flawless, true knowledge we need to finish our race strong! Proverbs 23:12 says that we are to commit ourselves to instruction (another translation could be "discipline") and attune our ears to hear words of knowledge. I don't want to sound like a broken record, but to get to know Him and His knowledge, we have to spend time with Him consistently. Just going to church and trying to cram it all in once a week is not sufficient if you really want to follow His training plan and run a strong race.

But just knowing isn't enough. I know that I should exercise and eat nutritious food if I want to keep my body healthy and strong, but it doesn't matter how much I know about staying healthy if I sit on the couch and stuff chips and candy bars into my mouth day after day.

God doesn't just want us to grow in Biblical knowledge. He wants us to be able to apply that knowledge and live it out on a daily basis, and that's wisdom. Second Peter 1 says that as we get to know Jesus better and better, His divine power will give us everything we need to live a Godly life. According to James 1:5, how do we receive this wisdom?

_____

All we have to do is ask! Proverbs 2:3 exhorts us to "cry out for insight, and ask for understanding." Through Jesus we have access to God's wisdom (1 Corinthians 1:30).

For the longest time, I read my Bible because that is what I was supposed to do. I did not really get much out of it. It was just a bunch of ancient words on a page that didn't really apply to me and the situations in my life. I would try to spend some time in the Word, aimlessly flip through the pages for a few days, and then give up. Now, each time I open my Bible, I pray that God's Word will be revealed to me in a way that I understand and can use in my life—that day.

Check where you feel you are when it comes to reading the Bible:

_____ Never open it.

_____ Just ancient words on a page.

_____ I am starting to understand that His word is wisdom for my life.

_____ I feel confident that each time I open the Bible, I will receive a Word that God wrote just for me and my circumstances.

If you checked either of the first two, don't feel that's where you will always be! I'm proof that God can turn "those ancient words on a page" into wisdom that applies to our circumstances. (But you do have to open the Bible to get there.)

Just as strengthening our running base causes helpful physical adaptations in our bodies, building up our relationship with Jesus and asking Him to reveal His wisdom makes it progressively easier to read the Bible and actually get something out of it.

Jesus wants to impart His wisdom to us through His Word! What an un-believable gift! The Creator of the universe, the foundation of our salvation, wants to spend time with us. He wants to teach us the wisdom we need to live a life that follows Him. Let's spend some time on our next run thanking Christ for being our "sure foundation." Then as we spend time with Him in His Word, let's ask Him to fill us with His wisdom.

Keep up your training! I am so excited for what God will share with you this week on your (easy paced!) runs!

Study Day Two

"Strengthen me, according to your word."
Psalm 119:28 (TNIV)

Let's start today off by learning about the awesome bodies our Lord created. Deep inside, we have muscles in our back, abdomen, hips, and pelvic floor that protect our spine and many of our internal organs. Our bodies' center of gravity is located here, and this is where all movement begins. These core muscles work together to keep us upright, and join to 29 other muscles to help stabilize us and create efficient movement. If these muscles are weak, our bodies do not work as effectively and we can injure easily. As a matter of fact, a major cause of lower back pain is weak core muscles.[10]

Most of us go about our daily lives without even using our core muscles. We sit slumped in our chairs, and stand with shoulders hunched and bellies hanging out. We don't even know the power we have when we simply engage those core muscles and allow them to do their job. But with a conscious decision, you can actively engage your core and use the strength and power it provides.

Engaging your core is a simple movement:

1. Stand up tall. Don't arch your back or stick your chin out. Think of your head sitting relaxed on top of your neck, with your shoulders relaxed and back.
2. Pull your belly button in toward your spine. You should feel your abdomen tighten.
3. Scoop your bottom underneath your hips.

Stand up and try that right now. How does it feel? _____

_____

_____

It might feel a little strange at first, but don't worry. The more you consciously engage your core, the more natural it will feel.

Even though it's a tiny movement, it requires thought and effort. Just walking around my house, I have to remind myself to engage my core. When I run, I consciously tell myself to engage my core. As I get tired, it's a constant battle to remember to pull my belly into my spine and stand up tall.

It is imperative that we not only learn how to engage our core, but also take the time to strengthen those muscles because core strength dictates so much of our movement, balance, and posture. Weak, unengaged core muscles will eventually cause other muscles to work improperly, causing injury.

Strengthening your core doesn't require hundreds of sit-ups a day. You don't need ripped, magazine-worthy abs to have a strong core. As a matter of fact, a person can have a great looking, washboard stomach and still have weak core muscles! Those washboard muscles are closer to the surface of your skin than the core muscles. That's why you can see them!

Many core exercises consist of very small movements. These small movements, done consistently over time, will result in a strong core that will give you power and balance when you need it most.

As a runner, I include core strengthening as part of my training program because no matter how strong my legs are or how many miles I log, if my core is weak, I'm not going to run as well or as far. It's these core muscles that I rely on when my legs get tired. My strength and power come from my core.

In Appendix C, I've included several exercises you can do to strengthen your core. I've also added core strengthening to your training schedule this week so that you can begin to incorporate these exercises in your training routine.

I need to have a strong spiritual core, as well, or the least little challenge can knock me down. Just like my physical core muscles, I need to devote time to building up and strengthening my core spiritual beliefs—the ones that keep me balanced and upright, regardless of my circumstances; and just like my core muscles, I have to learn how to activate these beliefs so I can stay strong.

Earlier this week, we discussed Christ as our foundation. He is the foundation, and there is nothing any of us can do to topple it. His foundation is complete and perfect. He finished it when He died on the cross. Through a relationship with Him, we have access to God's perfect wisdom and knowledge which we can apply to our daily lives.

What aspect of Day One seemed to impact you the most and why?

_____

_____

_____

_____

_____

If Christ is our foundation, what beliefs or core principles are we going to choose to build on that foundation? Are there some core beliefs that you hold so deeply that when you grow weary and weak they give you support?

Roll up your sleeves and get ready to dig into the Word because that's what we are going to do today—activate and strengthen our core with the Word.

Let's look at four core beliefs, or promises, that I cling to when I need strength. I have found that no matter what my circumstances, these truths encourage, strengthen, and bring me back to Christ. Read the core belief and then look up the Scripture that is tied to that belief. I want you to spend some time finding one more verse that backs up that truth. I want you to feel comfortable searching His Word for the truths that strengthen you!

If you're not sure how to go about finding verses on a subject, you can start by looking in the back of your Bible. They often have a "concordance," which is a list of topics or keywords (such as *love*) followed by a selection of verses that include that topic or keyword. If you prefer doing things online or want to see all verses with your keyword rather than just a selection of them, you can go to a site such as BibleGateway.com which lets you search the Bible by keyword or topic.

1. God loves me

Romans 8:35 _____

_____

_____

Romans 8:38-39 _____

_____

_____

Ephesians 3:17-19 _____

_____

_____

(My Verse) _____

_____

_____

God loves us! He loved us so much that He was willing to allow His son to be a sacrifice so that we may live. Nothing we can ever do can take away that love. When I am feeling particularly unlovely or when I feel the world is against me, I can hold on to the truth that God's love is so deep, so wide, and so high that nothing can separate me from His love.

2. God is good

Genesis 50:20 _____

_____

_____

Romans 8:28 _____

_____

_____

Titus 3:4-5 _____

_____

_____

James 5:11 _____

_____

_____

(My Verse) _____

_____

_____

When God revealed Himself to Moses in Exodus 34:6-7, He proclaimed He was merciful, gracious, forgiving, and overflowing with goodness. These words describe God's essence—His character—who He is. When bad things happen to us, He is there in His goodness to comfort us and turn that situation for His glory. When we—in our sinful nature—go against Him and fall, He is there in His mercy, full of forgiveness, to lift us up and set us on the right path again. No matter what happens around us or through us, His character is abounding in goodness and mercy.[11]

I can't help but think of a dear couple who have exemplified this core belief. When their oldest son was a teenager, he was killed in a car accident. They spent the next 20 years walking out Romans 8:28—that God uses all things for His goodness and His glory. They began a ministry in Ghana, building shelters for Christian tribesmen who were turned away from their tribe because of their new faith. They were invited to speak about their journey, and were able to help others who had lost children find God.

Then tragedy struck again, and their oldest daughter, now in her forties, was also killed in a car accident. I will never forget the words my friend cried the night she found out: "I've been through this once. I know how it feels to go through this. I don't want to do it again."

I watched them go through every emotion you can imagine that night and in the weeks to follow: from anger to grief to peace and back again. Yet all the while, they stood on God's goodness and mercy. Although they do not understand why they had to lose two children to car accidents, they continue to stand on the truth that God is good and that He will be glorified through their lives.

3. God hears my prayers and He wants *His* best for me

Psalm 4:3 _____

_____

_____

Psalm 17:6 _____

_____

_____

Psalm 102:17 _____

_____

_____

1 Peter 3:12 _____

_____

_____

(My Verse) _____

_____

_____

The phrases "hear my prayer" and "cry out" are repeated 74 times in the book of Psalms alone. The authors of the Psalms knew the power in crying out to God to hear their prayers, and we can be assured that if we cry out to God, He will hear our prayers as well. The book of Psalms show us that we can pray to God for anything, big or small, and that no emotion is off limits; but that does not always mean He will answer our prayers *the way* we want, *when* we want them answered.

For the longest time, I have cried out to God with a particular prayer. I begged and pleaded for Him to answer it. It seemed like a prayer after His heart, so why did He not answer me? As I struggled for understanding, I felt Him reveal to me that although my request wasn't out of line, my heart was. As I am lining up my heart with His will, He is answering my prayer—but in a way totally different than I had imagined! He knows what is best for us and has perfect timing. That leads us to:

4. God sees the big picture and has a perfect plan

Psalm 139:16 _____

_____

_____

Isaiah 46:9-10 _____

_____

_____

Jeremiah 29:11-13 _____

_____

_____

(My verse) _____

_____

_____

Last summer, we sent our oldest son to a two-week Christian summer camp that was a two-day drive away from our home. He really prefers to stay home, and is not fond of big loud crowds and lots of activity. We knew that this was going to be completely outside his comfort zone—and he informed us on a regular basis that he did not want to go and asked why we didn't understand.

It hurt me to see how much pain I was inflicting on him by forcing him to go to camp, but I could also see the bigger picture. I knew that after two or three days he would find a friend he could relate to and hang out with for the rest of camp; I knew that he would find a mentor in his counselors; and I knew that this camp had the potential to impact him spiritually, in a way that would carry through the rest of his life.

All he could see was being away from home with a bunch of strangers, and two parents who were being completely unfair. Dropping him off at camp—knowing he was scared and angry—was one of the hardest parenting days of my life. Two weeks later, we picked up a happy, spiritually stronger young man who won the camp's "most teachable" award. He now sees why we sent him and acknowledges his growth from the experience.

Has there been a time in your life when you saw the bigger picture and someone else did not? _____

_____

_____

_____

Can you think of a time when you did not see the bigger picture, but can see now that God did? _____

_____

_____

_____

God sees the beginning of time, the end of time, and my place in this little piece of it! I don't always know what He is orchestrating, but He knows how to get me where I need to go and when I need to be there. When I am frustrated with my situation, I remind myself that I can only see a tiny piece of God's puzzle, and through His Word, I know I can trust that He knows what He is doing.

5. God will never forsake me

Deuteronomy 31:8 _____

_____

_____

Psalm 9:10 _____

_____

_____

Psalm 27:10 _____

_____

_____

2 Corinthians 4:8-9 _____

_____

_____

(My Verse) _____

_____

_____

As long as we seek Him, we will never leave us. I may not always feel his presence, but His Word promises He is there. In a world where throwing away relationships is as common as taking out the trash, this may be a hard concept for some of us to really grasp; but I actually find this freeing! I can make mistakes; I can tell God how I really feel; I can show Him the deepest, darkest places of my heart and He will still stand by me. As you studied your Bible to find your own verse, you may have thought, *Yeah, but there seem to be a lot of verses where it looks like God did forsake His people.* Let's take a look at that for a minute.

Read 2 Chronicles 15:1-2 and 24:20. Throughout the Old Testament, the people of Israel abandoned God over and over. They worshipped false gods. They begged for human kings to lead them rather than the prophets God appointed. They took matters into their own hands rather than waiting for God to act. Now read Deuteronomy 30:1-5. Through it all, God patiently waited for His people to return to Him. God is a gentleman; He never pushes Himself on us, but rather waits for us to seek His presence, guidance, and forgiveness. He is not going to force us to do what is right in His eyes—we get to make that choice. We turn away from Him, and God waits patiently for us to return. His actions and His words show us that even when we go astray, all it takes is the tiniest movement back to Him and He is there with open arms to love us and bless us.

Whew! I know that was a lot of Scripture to look up! I hope you were able to stick with it and persevere. I also hope you took the time to find your own verses for each of those core beliefs, and we have only scratched the surface! There are so many incredible truths and promises we can stand on in the Word, and so many verses we can use to help us remain strong. As we continue in our study, we will add to these four promises.

I challenge you to come back to these pages when your road gets bumpy and training gets tough. Let these truths strengthen you! Make a conscious choice to pull in your belly, stand up tall and strengthen your core—physically and spiritually.

I look forward to spending time with you next week on the pages of this study!

Week 3

Moving Forward in Faith

After completing this week's training and homework you will be able to:

- demonstrate your faith by your actions—physically and spiritually—even when you can't see results,
- patiently let the training plan unfold rather than trying to take things in your own hands and rush, and
- find the flaw(s) in your excuses and get rid of them.

Study Day One

> *We walk by faith, not by sight.*
> 2 Corinthians 5:7 (NKJV)

Can you believe that this week you will be running seven miles on your long run? For some of you, that may be the longest you have ever run before! If you have done the training and have been building your training foundation, *have faith that you are ready.* Just remember to keep an easy pace—and even stop and walk, if necessary. The key is to finish. It doesn't matter how long it takes you!

This week we are going to continue to build on what we have learned over the past couple of weeks. We've talked a lot about God's Word; how it is our training plan, full of wisdom and knowledge. Through Jesus, we have access to that wisdom and knowledge which can build us up and strengthen us. I hope you have incorporated a few of the core exercises from Appendix B into your training routine. Even a few minutes, twice a week, will make a huge difference in your core strength.

Usually around Week 3 of my training, weariness and doubt begin to creep in—especially if I had a couple of bad training runs in the previous weeks. The newness of the training has worn off and the race seems so far away that it isn't quite real. The idea of running a half marathon doesn't seem so fun anymore. I start to wonder if I can complete the training—and why I even want to try. Is it really worth it?

Perhaps you're not seeing significant improvements in your training yet, so you're beginning to wonder if it really works. Maybe you're finding it harder and harder to lace up your shoes each day to do the training. It can seem like so much effort! Or maybe the process is getting boring.

Is there anything about training that is hard for you right now?

_____

_____

Has there been a day (or even days) that you've thought about quitting the training?

_____

It's now that you need to dig deeply and rely on the training program. You need to stick with the plan and continue to move forward—even when you

Week 3 TRAINING SCHEDULE

*There are 5 workouts (4 runs, 1 cross training) and 2 rest days each week.
The workout days are flexible, however use 1 rest day after your longest run.*

WEEK 3	WORKOUT 1	WORKOUT 2	WORKOUT 3	WORKOUT 4	WORKOUT 5	WORKOUT 6	WORKOUT 7
PLAN	Easy Run 40 min	X-train 30 min + 20 min core	Easy Run 35 min	Easy Run 45 min + 10 min core	Rest	Long Run 7 miles	Rest
LOG							

Always spend 5-10 minutes warming up and 5-10 minutes cooling down. This can be included in your total time/mileage.

Long Run: These should be at an easy, conversational pace.
Easy Run: Easy runs should be at an easy, conversational pace. On a scale of 1-10 (10 being all out effort), an easy run should feel like a 5-6.
X-train: Cross-training. Anything other than running, such as swimming, biking, walking, strength training.
LOG: This is where you write what you ACTUALLY did that day, along with a description of how you prepared and how you felt.
Core: Choose a few core exercises and spend time strengthening your core after your run.

We walk by faith, not by sight. — 2 CORINTHIANS 5:7 (NKJV)

(This page is left blank so that you can cut out the workout plan on the other side and display it where you'll see it regularly.)

don't feel like it—trusting that if you follow the plan, you will succeed. It's more than just *believing* that it's a good training plan. You have to put those running shoes on and *do the mileage*, week after week, even when you'd rather sit on the couch (or stay in bed).

Remember last week when I listed the physical adaptations that occur as we train? These adaptations prepare our bodies for longer and longer runs. We can't necessarily feel those changes. I can't see capillaries increasing in number in my muscles. I can't feel my body learning to use fat as an energy source. I simply have to believe that those things are happening as I continue to train.

The word translated as "faith" in our English Bibles is *pistis* in the original Greek, meaning belief or conviction.[1] Hebrews 11:1 describes what our faith—our beliefs and convictions—does for us. Read Hebrews 11:1 and write your understanding of its meaning.

_____

_____

_____

_____

In fact, Hebrews 11:6 tells us that without faith, it is impossible to please God; but faith is more than just *believing* in God. James 2:19 says that even the demons believe in God. Faith requires some sort of movement that brings us closer to God. *Faith* is an action word. Beth Moore says a "walk of faith assumes a walk with God. Faith cannot walk alone … Faith is the primary means by which we place our hand in the outstretched hand of God and join Him."[2] Faith is not a feeling. Our faith helps us *overcome* our feelings!

Paul is encouraging the believers in Corinth to a more spiritual life when he says in 2 Corinthians 5:7, "We walk by faith, not by sight" (NKJV). *Walk*, in this sense, means "to live" or "conduct one's self."[3] In other words, we are to live our lives, to conduct ourselves, by our faith—not by what we see with our eyes.

Hebrews 11 is a "faith in action" chapter, filled with accounts of Old Testament men and women who lived their lives by faith and gained approval from God (Hebrews 11:2). Let's learn about some of these men and women and how they triumphed in their faith walk. Their stories will encourage us to continue our own faith walk!

Enoch

Read Genesis 5:21-24 and Hebrews 11:5.

Not much is said about Enoch in the Old Testament. All we really know about him is that at the age of 65, he began to walk faithfully with God, and continued to walk with God up until the day God took him into His presence. Notice that the Bible doesn't say that Enoch died; it says that God took him into his presence! Walking faithfully with God was all Enoch needed to do to gain the kind of incredible approval from God—never having to experience death—that we only read about happening to one other person in the entire Bible: the prophet Elijah!

Noah

Read Genesis 6:9, 6:22, 7:5 and Hebrews 11:7.

Because Noah walked with God and was obedient throughout his extremely long life (he lived to be 950!), he and his family were saved from the great flood that wiped out the earth. Reread Hebrews 11:7 and write it here:

_____

_____

_____

God warned Noah about "things not yet seen" (NIV). Noah built the ark in the middle of a desert, without a drop of water for miles around. Talk about walking by faith, not by sight! Considering that the rest of the world was corrupt and wicked, I am sure Noah found himself the subject of much ridicule. And think about the expense of all the materials he used!

There was a lot of risk in building that boat. Walking in faith requires risk. It requires stepping into the moment with God, knowing only He can see His plan for you. Noah risked his reputation and his finances to build the ark.

Consider the following comments and check the one that most closely resembles your walk with God right now:

_____ I wake up each day determined to walk with God.

_____ I walk my own way, and God is welcome to join me.

_____ I have never really given walking with God much thought.

_____ I try to walk with God, but I keep stumbling.

_____ I would like to walk with God, but I'm afraid of what my friends and family will say!

I have to admit that, for most of my life, I walked my own way and asked God to join me. You may have uttered this prayer yourself in the past: "God, I am going to _____ [fill in the blank with some decision]. Please bless it!" But for the last couple of years, I have truly done my best to wake up each day determined to follow what God had for me that day rather than my own plan.

I can't say it has always been easy. A lot of times my friends and family have looked at me like I have bugs crawling out of my ears. I have even caught a few of the "She's gone crazy" glances between people that they didn't mean for me to see. Honestly, some days, I'm not really sure what path God has for me. That's when I go back to His Word, seek Him in prayer, and continue to draw close to Him and His promises. I build up my faith with the core principles we discussed last week—that He is good, loves me, wants the very best for me, and will never forsake me.

I don't have to be perfect in my walk! Isn't that great news? My own sinful nature (in forms such as pride, selfishness, and stubbornness) causes me to stumble at times; but even Noah was far from perfect. Genesis 9:20-24 finds Noah drunk and naked in his tent. God doesn't expect perfection; He simply requires that we continue to walk with Him. Even though Noah made mistakes, he remained faithful to God throughout his entire life. Noah crossed his finish line, not as a perfect person, but as one who was faithful to the end. That's the path that I choose!

Abraham and Sarah

Read Genesis 12:1-4, 15:5-6, 17:16-27, 22:1-10; and Hebrews 11:8-12, 11:17-19.

Here is a couple I can relate to! Throughout the course of their very long lives, Abraham and Sarah show moments of fear and doubt, and even take matters into their own hands instead of waiting for God's promises.

Walking faithfully with God requires movement. He doesn't want us to stay where we are. For us, it may not mean a physical move, but being willing to try things in new ways. For Abraham, it meant physically moving his family to a new land. Then, as Abraham and Sarah settled in their new strange land, fear set in. Rather than trust God for their safety (after all, He was the one who told them to move there!), they lied about being husband and wife to avoid the possibility of being killed—not just once, but twice![4] Isn't it easy to allow fear to take over while in the midst of following God? It is so hard to walk an unknown path that only God can see! It takes faith to believe that He will come through on His promises for those who seek Him!

Take a moment now to read Genesis 16:1-4. This is the part of Abraham and Sarah's story that I most relate to. God had promised in Genesis 15:5 that Abraham and Sarah would have descendants as numerous as the stars in the sky; but as the years passed and Sarah was still childless, *she decided to help God with His promise.* She gave her servant to Abraham as another wife, and allowed her to bear him a child. Rather than wait for God's promises, she took matters into her own hands.

Has there ever been a time you became impatient with God and decided to take matters into your own hands?

_____

_____

_____

_____

It's so easy to stop trusting God and try to manipulate the situation for the outcome we want! God has a "best" plan for us; and when we take matters into our own hands, we may have a *good* plan, but it is not His *best*. Part of walking with God is being willing to wait for His plan. Remember, one of the core beliefs we can stand on is that God's picture is bigger than ours. He knows all of the things that have to come together for His plan to be fulfilled.

I think Abraham's walk in faith is exemplified best when God commanded him to sacrifice Isaac, as told in Genesis 22. God called Abraham, and Abraham's response was, "Here I am." Abraham did not try to bargain or do it his own way first. He simply obeyed. Maybe after doing things the hard way for so many years, he finally realized that God's way was the best way. I can't even imagine the inner turmoil Abraham must have felt, knowing he was being asked to sacrifice his one and only son to prove his obedience to God. He was prepared to kill Isaac to prove his love for God, but continued to listen and was obedient when, at the last second, God shouted for him to stop.

Although the sacrifices God has required of me are not as severe as having to sacrifice my child, there have been things in my life that I have felt God telling me to give up. It's not always easy to follow His path. He sometimes asks us to make painful sacrifices. He never promised an easy, pain-free life, but walking faithfully with God provides us with blessings that far outweigh anything we may have to give up. Hebrews 10:35 says "So do not throw away this confident trust in the Lord. Remember the great reward it brings you!"

Don't get discouraged if your training seems hard this week. Just keep moving, even if you don't see any progress! That is moving in faith!

Study Day Two

There is a proper time and procedure for every matter.
Ecclesiastes 8:6 (NIV)

Welcome back! I am so proud of you for sticking with this program and your training. I just know that God will bless your efforts, both physically and spiritually.

As you move forward in your training, be sure to stick with your warm ups, cool downs, and stretching. It's easy to forget the basics, or to think that this aspect of training isn't as important anymore; but the basics are as important today as they were when you first started. Don't forget that you can include your warm up and cool down in your training time and mileage. Your body needs those important steps.

Remember, warming up gradually prepares your body for a more intense workout by filling your muscles with oxygen-rich blood. I find that my best runs are those where I spend a good 10 minutes gradually warming up to my training pace.

Cooling down allows your body to gradually return to its normal state. Your body has distributed most of its blood to your legs and other running muscles, and that blood needs to return back to all of your organs. If you don't allow ample time to cool down before you come to a complete stop, you risk becoming light-headed and experiencing a significant drop in blood pressure. It is so easy to justify skipping these steps, especially as your training runs get longer and you feel the need to save some time. Don't!

Just like short-changing your training by skipping proper warm up and cool down, it is easy to short change spending time in God's Word when life gets busy or your quiet time seems routine. Guard against this tendency. This is a basic step in your Christian walk that is necessary to grow your faith.

We spent the first part of this week getting to know some of the faithful men and women of the Bible. Of the men and women we learned about, who do you most relate to and why?

_____

_____

_____

We have one more hero of faith to learn about today to encourage us on our own faith walk.

Moses
Read Exodus 2:1-6, 3:1-4 and Hebrews 11:23-28.
God had a plan for Moses from the very beginning, which He revealed to him in the burning bush. Read Exodus 3:11, 13; 4:1, 10, 13 to see Moses' responses to God's plans. What are some of the excuses Moses used to explain why he couldn't do what God had planned for him? _____

_____

Moses tried every argument in the book! "No one will listen to me. Who am I to lead people? No one is going to believe me! I'm not a good speaker. Please send someone else!"

What excuses have you used in your faith walk? Has there been a time when you used an excuse to get out of being obedient to God? _____

_____

_____

_____

Now think about your physical training. What excuses have stopped you from following your plan? _____

_____

_____

Let's take a look at Moses' excuses again. What do they all have in common?

_____

_____

They all center around "me" and "I." They all seem sort of selfish, don't they? His excuses center around himself and what he can and can't do or what he does and doesn't want. But God says, *I am bigger than what you can and can't do. I have a plan for you! Trust in me and I will give you all that you need to walk on My path. Just trust me for the things you can't see.* "I will be with you" (Exodus 3:12). God's "I" is so much bigger than our "I," just as His eyes see so much more than ours!

God gave Moses the tools and the words needed to follow Him, right when Moses needed them. Moses stepped out in faith each time God gave him a new command. As he saw God was there to meet him, his faith grew.

Moses isn't the only one.

Moses gives me hope! I also have times when I ask God, "Who am I? I am not good at what you are calling me to do! Please...I don't want to do what you are asking me to do!" But we aren't the only people involved. When we refuse to walk the path God intended for us out of fear or selfishness, other people's lives are greatly diminished. We impact other people just as Moses' obedience impacted the freedom of God's chosen people. Through Moses' testimony, I know that God will give me the resources I need, when I need them, if I remain obedient and continue to walk with Him.

The more we walk in faith, the more obedient we will become. The faithful men and women of the Bible, the heroes of Hebrews 11, inspire us to be encouraged by our past, move confidently in the present, and hope for our unseen future. I want to live my life walking with God—each step more obedient—gaining His approval. Don't you?

Where is God calling you to walk in faith? He may not be telling you to move your family to a foreign land or sacrifice your child, but do you feel Him telling you to give up something you love? To trust Him in an area of your life where you have tried to walk alone? He wants to lead you, but you have to be ready and willing to follow. Not sure if God is really calling you to follow a certain path? Fill yourself with His Word so you can learn to recognize His leading. He will not stray from His promises.

This week as you train, possibly into mileage that you have never before experienced, ask God to lead you in your faith walk with Him.

I know the last couple of weeks have been intense. I am excited to see what blessings will arise out of your willingness to grow in faith.

Our Bodies as Temples

After completing this week's training and homework, you will be able to:

* understand the relationship between the Temple of the Old Testament and our physical bodies,
* recognize that our minds, souls and bodies are made to glorify God,
* know how to make appropriate food choices for before, during, and after your runs, and
* have the proper tools to combat tummy issues that might arise.

Study Day One

> *Don't you realize that your body is the temple of the Holy Spirit, who lives in you and was given to you by God? You do not belong to yourself, for God bought you with a high price. So you must honor God with your body.*
> 1 Corinthians 6:19-20

Can you believe it? This week marks one whole month we've been training together! Take a few minutes to look back through your training logs for the last three weeks. Isn't it inspiring to see where you started and where you are now? Can you see any patterns—good or bad—in your workouts that you can use to improve your training?

_____

_____

_____

_____

I recently moved from basically flat ground at sea level to a very hilly area at an elevation of 5,400 feet. I was in the middle of training for a marathon, and my long runs were up to 15 miles before I moved. When I went on my first run a couple of days after moving, I thought my lungs and quads were going to explode! Gasping for breath, I barely made it 3 miles. Air is less dense at higher altitude, so you take in less oxygen with each breath. Your body has to go through a process of creating a higher concentration of red blood cells and hemoglobin to make up for the lack of oxygen in the air.[1] This process takes a few weeks, and even though I knew I would acclimate eventually, I have to admit I was pretty discouraged. I began the slow process of retraining for the marathon.

Several months later my training was still pretty tough, and some days I wondered if it would ever be easy again. While unpacking, I came across my training log for another marathon a year before. This particular training plan had been very intense because I had specific goals I wanted to reach in my running. Looking back through my workouts gave me such hope! I saw good runs and bad runs, speedy runs and slow runs. Seeing how much I progressed in that training program gave me the reassurance that I if I stick with it, my training will get easier—even at altitude. The message is clear: Don't underestimate the power of your training log! If you have not been diligent about filling it out so far, make a commitment to yourself to fill it out consistently over the next two months.

Week 4 TRAINING SCHEDULE

There are 5 workouts (4 runs, 1 cross training) and 2 rest days each week.
The workout days are flexible, however use 1 rest day after your longest run.

WEEK 4	WORKOUT 1	WORKOUT 2	WORKOUT 3	WORKOUT 4	WORKOUT 5	WORKOUT 6	WORKOUT 7
PLAN	Easy Run 35 min	X-train 30 min + 20 min core	Easy Run 35 min	Easy Run 40 min + 10 min core	Rest	Long Run 5 miles	Rest
LOG							

Always spend 5-10 minutes warming up and 5-10 minutes cooling down. This can be included in your total time/mileage.

Long Run: These should be at an easy, conversational pace.
Easy Run: Easy runs should be at an easy, conversational pace. On a scale of 1-10 (10 being all out effort), an easy run should feel like a 5-6.
X-train: Cross-training. Anything other than running, such as swimming, biking, walking, strength training.
LOG: This is where you write what you ACTUALLY did that day, along with a description of how you prepared and how you felt.
Core: Choose a few core exercises and spend time strengthening your core after your run.

Don't you realize that your body is the temple of the Holy Spirit, who lives in you and was given to you by God? You do not belong to yourself, for God bought you with a high price. So you must honor God with your body. — 1 CORINTHIANS 6:19-20

(This page is left blank so that you can cut out the workout plan on the other side and display it where you'll see it regularly.)

If you look at this week's training program you will notice that your long run has dropped back to 5 miles. Cutting back your mileage this week will give your body a chance to recover and repair from last week's long run. I always include a recovery week every fourth week in training programs. This ratio of building weeks to recovery weeks reduces injury and allows for stronger running overall.

Physical and spiritual nutrition

Today we are going shift our focus to a topic near and dear to my heart: our physical bodies, nutrition, and how this relates to God. I will also give you lots of tips for eating while training; what to eat, when to eat it, and how to avoid common tummy issues while running.

As I study anatomy, exercise physiology, and nutrition, I grow more and more amazed at the wonder of our bodies. God created an intricate, complex, orderly masterpiece when He created humans. Have you noticed how natural it is to accept the existence of God when you see majestic snow-capped mountains against a crystal blue sky, or a spectacular sunrise glinting over the ocean at the beach? That's how I feel when I study the inner workings of the human body, and discover how all of the systems work perfectly together—down to the tiniest cell. Our bodies truly are "fearfully and wonderfully made" (Psalm 139:14).

Genesis 2:7 details exactly how we were created. "Then the LORD God formed the man from the dust from the ground. He breathed the breath of life into the man's nostrils, and man became a living person." I get an image in my head of the Creator of the universe, our heavenly Father, lovingly and gently sculpting His most precious creation—the the only one patterned after His own image according to Genesis 1:27—out of the dust of the earth. Our physical bodies were created first, to house our spirits.

In his book *Heaven*, Randy Alcorn describes it this way:

> God did not create Adam as a spirit and place it inside a body. Rather, he first created a body, *then* breathed into it a spirit. There was never a moment when a human existed without a body. Neurophysiological studies reveal an intimate connection between the body and what has historically been referred to as the soul—which includes the mind, emotions, will, intentionality, and capacity to worship. It appears that we are not essentially spirits who inhabit bodies but we are essentially as much physical as we are spiritual. We cannot be fully human without both a spirit *and* a body.[2]

It seems to me that we have somehow disconnected our spirits from our bodies. We work on our spiritual lives while neglecting the physical, or we strengthen our physical bodies without regard for our spiritual health. But God intended for us to turn everything over to Him.

Read 1 Thessalonians 5:23. What did Paul say we are to keep blameless (or preserved)?

_____

_____

Read 1 Corinthians 6:19-20. Write these verses in your own words, below:

_____

_____

_____

_____

What did Paul mean when he called our bodies a temple of the Holy Spirit in 1 Corinthians 6:19? After Moses led the Israelites out of Egypt, God sent for him at Mount Sinai. God told Moses, "I want the people of Israel to build me a sacred residence where I can live among them. You must make this tabernacle and its furnishings exactly according to the plans I will show you" (Exodus 25:9). For forty days and nights, God gave Moses exact, detailed instructions. Exodus chapters 25 through 31 list the instructions given to Moses, down to the very last detail.

What were some of the materials God required, according to Exodus 25:3?

_____

_____

_____

Pretty high quality materials, don't you think? God wanted His dwelling place to remind the Israelites of His glory—that He is highest, most exalted, and worthy of worship.

Fast forward to 970 B.C., at the end of King David's reign. God is still dwelling in the Tabernacle, now located in Jerusalem. David crowns his son, Solomon, as king of Israel and begins work on the plans for the building of God's Temple (see 2 Samuel 7:12-13 and 1 Chronicles 28:10).

Read 1 Chronicles 22:14-16 and 28:11-18 and write down a few of the instructions King David gave Solomon regarding the building of the Temple:

_____

_____

_____

_____

And that's just the tip of the iceberg! Chapter after chapter of the Old Testament describes in detail how the Temple was to be constructed and how it was to be maintained. According to 1 Chronicles 28:19, where did these directions come from?

When the time came for Solomon to begin the building of the Temple, he was very careful to build it to his father's specifications. How long did it take King Solomon to finish the Temple (1 Kings 6:38)?

How long had Solomon been king at this point?

It took a long time before the Temple was finally finished and God had His dwelling place. Think about it! King David began the planning over 11 years before it was complete.

Once the Temple was finished it became the centerpiece of the Jewish culture. Jews made long and dangerous pilgrimages to the Temple three times a year in obedience to God's Word. They sacrificed animals at the Temple to atone for their sins. The Temple was the one and only place they could be physically close to God.

Let's move through history some more and flip over to the tiny book of Haggai, almost at the end of the Old Testament. The year is now around 520 B.C. The Temple lay in ruins, destroyed by the armies of Babylon some 66 years earlier. Although King Cyrus had allowed the exiled Jews to return to Jerusalem in 535 B.C. to rebuild the Temple, they had gotten sidetracked.

Read Haggai 1:3-6. How was life unfolding for the Jews?

Things weren't going so well, were they? Read on in Haggai 1:7-9. The Jews had neglected to rebuild God's dwelling place, instead focusing on their own houses and fields. Haggai urged the Jews to refocus their priorities and build God the Temple He deserved.

Haggai 2:18-19 shows what happened when the Jews made God's Temple a priority in their lives: The day they laid the foundation, God promised to bless them from that day forward. He did not wait until the Temple was complete. He was eager to bless them the minute they showed the tiniest bit of obedience and made Him a priority.

I actually had the opportunity to visit Israel and stand on the Temple Mount. Although the Temple is again in ruins and most of its walls are buried deep underground, the size and splendor is still inspiring. In it's finest glory it would have been breath-taking.

What does this have to do with our bodies?

Through Christ's death and resurrection, we are no longer bound by Old Testament laws to make pilgrimages or sacrifice animals. God no longer dwells in a man-made structure. According to 1 John 4:13-15, where does God reside now?

_____

_____

Through the gift of the Holy Spirit, God now dwells inside each of us. Matthew McNutt, a pastor and contestant on *The Biggest Loser* television show, has this to say about God's Temple:

> What jumped out at me...was the overwhelming number of scriptures throughout the Old Testament speaking to the sacredness, holiness, importance, and care of the temple. Those passages aren't there as some sort of history lesson—they still apply today. In fact, I firmly believe that one of the primary purposes of the Old Testament temple was to prepare us for the incredible privilege and responsibility it is for our bodies to now serve as temples![3]

I just love how God connects the Old Testament with the New Testament! Shirer, Moore, and Arthur say in their study of King David, "We are the modern-day tabernacles in which God's presence dwells."[4] Our bodies belong to God—He bought them with the blood of Christ.

The Tabernacle and the Old Testament laws reminded God's chosen people that He was the one who delivered them from slavery and that He had authority in their lives. We are no longer bound by the Old Testament laws that told the Israelites what they were allowed to eat, how the food was to be prepared, and when they were to eat it. We must remember, though, that even with our freedom in this, "whether you eat or drink, or whatever you do, do it all for the glory of God" (1Corinthians 10:31).

Leslie Fields says, "How shall we use our freedom in Christ? If it ends in mindless consumption, exploitation of God's gifts, and mistreatment of our bodies, then we have allowed our appetites to enslave us again."[5] God absolutely cares about how we treat our bodies, just as He cared about how the Israelites treated the Temple building. As Paul told the church in 1 Corinthians 10:23, we may have the *right* to do something, but that doesn't mean it's beneficial to do so.

In a society where rail-thin airbrushed models are the images of perfection, where 68% of the American population 20 years and over struggles with being overweight or obese[6], and up to 10 million have eating disorders[7], the subject of fitness and nutrition is tricky at best. I have been labeled "insensitive" when voicing my opinions on exercise and healthy eating. Nothing could be further from my heart. I simply want people to take a look at their eating and exercise habits. Are they offering those areas of their lives to the Lord? God isn't concerned about a perfect body or the perfect weight, but he does have requirements about our bodies. Look up Romans 6:13 and write it here:

_____

_____

_____

I eat reasonable portions of nutritious food because I want what I put into my mouth to strengthen my body—the Lord's dwelling place. I exercise and take care of my body because I want it to work to the best of its ability, and to be physically ready when God calls me to act. If my whole body is to be used as a tool to do what is right for God, then I have a responsibility to take care of it. That doesn't mean I never eat cake or drink a soda. As Lisa Bevere says in *You Are Not What You Weigh,* "When it is time to celebrate, I enjoy food. But I eat to celebrate—not to celebrate eating."[8]

It is very easy to become legalistic about nutrition and exercise. As a matter of fact, there is a new eating disorder, *orthorexia nervosa* or just orthorexia, in which a person becomes so obsessed with eating healthily that it consumes them. They become self-righteous, reaching the point of pitying or even feeling disdain for anyone who does not follow their "pure" diet. When temptation gets the best of them and they eat something not on their list of allowed foods, they are racked with guilt and self-condemnation.[9] When I read about orthorexia, I could not help but think about the Pharisees in Jesus' time who were so obsessed with obeying the law that they ignored the message of God's grace.

It is easy to let food and exercise become an idol. I know this because I have struggled with it, both with food and with exercise. An idol is "anything you draw your strength from or give your strength to. It is how you spend your self—your time, your efforts, your thoughts."[10]

Let's make sure that God remains foremost in our thoughts as we spend the rest of our time this week discovering healthier eating habits and how to fuel our bodies appropriately for running.

Study Day Two

"Therefore, I urge you, brothers and sisters, in view of God's mercy, to offer your bodies as a living sacrifice, holy and pleasing to God—this is true worship. Do not conform to the pattern of this world, but be transformed by the renewing of your mind. Then you will be able to test and approve what God's will is—his good, pleasing and perfect will."
Romans 12:1-2 (TNIV)

I hope Day One gave you some food for thought! Our bodies are amazing creations from God, and we should take care of them to the best of our ability. As a quick review, write 1 Corinthians 6:19-20 and 1 Corinthians 10:31 here:

_____

_____

_____

_____

Today we will spend some time learning how to apply those verses to our lives in a practical way. Some of my guidelines for a healthier lifestyle may be old news to you, while others might be something you have never before considered. Please keep in mind that these are simply guidelines, not law. Just like a buffet, if it seems to make sense to you, try it. If it doesn't appeal to you, feel free to leave it!

1) Stop drinking sugary drinks and replace them with water. Sugary drinks include sodas, sweet teas, and juices. If you choose to apply only one guideline to your life, this should be the one! I personally believe that a huge contributor to the obesity problem in America, especially in children, is the amount of sugar we consume in the form of drinks. A whopping 43% of all the sugar we take in comes from drinks; 33% in the form of soda, 10% in the form of sweetened juices.[11]

The American Heart Association (AHA) recommends that women should consume no more than 100 calories, or 6 teaspoons, of added sugar per day. Men should consume no more than 150 calories, or nine teaspoons.[12] Now compare that to the fact that a typical 12 ounce can of cola has approximately 10 teaspoons of sugar in it (mostly in the form of high fructose corn syrup) and about 140 calories! If you have a hard time picturing just how much sugar that really is, stack ten sugar cubes in a glass. Just one 12 oz. soda pushes you beyond the AHA's recommendations for an entire day!

How many sugary drinks does your family drink per day? Don't forget to include juice boxes, flavored waters, juice, soda, and energy or sports drinks.

_____ We don't drink soda at our house

_____ We consume about 1 liter of soda/juice boxes per day

_____ We consume more than 1 liter of sugary drinks per day

I no longer purchase sugary drinks for my family. Instead, I bought some thermoses and pack ice water in my kids' lunches. We no longer order sodas with our meals at restaurants. The money we save (with 5 people ordering drinks at a restaurant, it easily adds $12.00 to the tab!) helps me buy organic items at the grocery store, which tend to be a bit more expensive. The next time you go to the store, add up the cost of all the drinks you have in your cart—juices, energy drinks, teas, and sodas. Your grocery bill (and belly size) will go down considerably when you leave those drinks on the shelves.

2) Become aware of what you are putting into your body. When you grocery shop, do you have a habit of reading the ingredients list and nutritional information on the food you put in your cart?

(Circle one:)   Yes   No   Sometimes, but it's not a habit

Look up Proverbs 15:14 and write it here:

_____

_____

We can't make wise choices if we don't know what's in our food! It never dawned on me to read the labels of the foods I was feeding my family until I read a few books about nutrition. Reading food labels takes a bit more time at the store but it is well worth it for my family's health. You cannot rely on the "healthy" claims on the front of the food packaging. The truth is in the ingredients, not the advertising! There have been a few times when I was in a rush, didn't read the ingredients, and thought I was making good, healthy choices based on the packaging—only to come home and find out that the foods I thought were healthy were really full of unhealthy, unnatural ingredients.

Just because a product is labeled "healthy" or "all natural" does not mean it actually is. There are very loose regulations on how food manufacturers can advertise their products. The only way to determine if a product is truly healthy is to read the nutritional information. When it comes to ingredients, simpler is better. If a food has a list of 10–20 different ingredients, many of which have long, scientific names, I really don't think I want it in my body. I want foods that have a short list of recognizable ingredients.

Two ingredients that rarely make their way into my shopping cart are high fructose corn syrup and hydrogenated oils. I could spend another three pages writing about the dangers of these two ingredients alone. Rather than bore you with the details, it boils down to this: they are man-made chemicals that our bodies do not know how to metabolize properly. They cause a multitude of health issues and should rarely, if ever be consumed.

I challenge you to really read the ingredients of the foods you are purchasing the next time you are at the store. Become educated about what you put into your body.

3) Learn the nutritional content of the foods at the restaurants you frequent. Most restaurant chains have a list of nutritional information somewhere on their website. Be sure to pay attention to the serving sizes. One of my favorite restaurants lists their entrées as feeding 3 people! That means the calories per serving have to be multiplied by 3 if you eat the entire dish. I was shocked when I learned that if I ate my favorite entrée by myself, I would be eating over 1000 calories in one meal! Some better options are to share a meal with someone, or ask for a to-go box with your meal and immediately put half of it in the to-go box before you begin eating. If you do choose to splurge and eat your favorite high calorie meal, make the decision to forgo an appetizer or dessert.

4) Take snacks with you while running errands. That way when you or the kids gets hungry, you're not tempted to stop at the nearest fast food restaurant or convenience store. I have a little cooler that I pack with cheese sticks, fresh fruit, dried fruits and nuts, organic granola bars, organic crackers, and water for hungry tummies on the road. It takes an extra five minutes to pack before I head out the door but it is so worth it! I save money and I know our snacks are healthier than french fries or chips and a soda.

These are just a few of the guidelines I implemented as my family began to recognize that we have a responsibility to God's dwelling place. Of the guidelines listed above, are there any that you already follow? _____

_____

_____

If not, are there one or two you would be willing to implement over the next two months? _____

_____

_____

Please do not misinterpret what I am saying. God's new covenant is paved with grace and mercy. I know that I cannot "eat myself healthy" into heaven. But as we grow in the knowledge of Christ and of the responsibilities we have as children of the Most High, our road narrows in every aspect of our lives. The ways of the world can no longer be our path.

I think as Christians we easily recognize that we need to guard what we feed our minds and spirits. I claim without hesitation that we need to take that one step further and guard what we feed our bodies as well. Again, I am not speaking of legalism—just awareness and knowledge. Most of us have never had the inclination to turn our eating habits over to the Lord. I certainly didn't. I followed the ways of the world, blindly eating what pleased my flesh. Since Adam and Eve took the first bite of that tempting, forbidden fruit, the ways of the world have led to death. As Paul urged His brothers and sisters in Rome, I urge you as well:

"Therefore, I urge you, brothers and sisters, in view of God's mercy, to offer your bodies as a living sacrifice, holy and pleasing to God—this is your true and proper worship. Do not conform to the pattern of this world, but be transformed by the renewing of your mind. Then you will be able to test and approve what God's will is—His good, pleasing and perfect will" (Romans 12:1-2, TNIV).

Whew! I am sure that is a lot to digest. I promise, the rest of today will be less heavy. (And you won't have to answer many questions!)Let's spend the rest of our time together discussing some practical ways to feed our bodies as we train. To start, let's see how running affects our nutrition.

An average, 150 pound person typically burns 100 calories per mile. If you weigh more than that, you will burn more calories, if you weigh less, you will burn less. As an example, let's say a 150 pound person ran 3 miles. He or she will have burned about 300 calories. That's about the calories in a regular sized Snickers® bar.

Why do I even mention this? Sometimes training for an endurance race gives people the false belief that they can eat whatever they want, or that they can eat in larger quantities than normal.

While you may not burn as many calories as you thought during your runs, there are some secondary benefits. One of these is an effect called excess post-exercise oxygen consumption (EPOC), which causes your body's metabolic rate to remain elevated for hours after you stop running. This means your body burns more calories after you run than before you ran.[13]

Remember that I said in the introduction that weight loss should not be a goal of this program, nor should it be expected. I have never lost weight training for a race—not even my 50K. In fact, trying to lose a lot of weight while training will be a detriment to running your best race. Your body needs energy to run, and it can only get that energy if you eat enough of the right foods.

So how do we get that much-needed fuel without eating more calories than we burn? I am going to break down nutritional guidelines by run length. These are just guidelines; everyone has different metabolism and different energy needs. If you find these guidelines are not meeting your needs, tweak them a little until you find what works for you.

Runs less than an hour

Typically you have enough energy stored in your body to fuel a run that lasts less than an hour.

What to eat before your run:
If you are going to run before breakfast or late in the day before dinner, you will find you have more energy if you eat a small snack at least an hour before you run. A small snack might be one of these:

69

- a piece of toast with a tablespoon of peanut butter
- half an english muffin and a spoonful of jam
- two tablespoons hummus and a handful of carrots or a small pita
- a handful of pretzels dipped in peanut butter
- 8 ounces of sports drink
- half a bagel with a tablespoon of cream cheese or a piece of cheese
- a cheese stick with a banana

Be sure to drink 8-16 ounces of water with your snack.

What to eat during your run:
Your body usually won't need anything but water during a run less than an hour. I usually carry a water bottle on any run over 4 miles and drink 2-4 ounces every fifteen minutes or so. If the weather is warm and I am sweating a lot, I drink closer to 4 ounces every fifteen minutes to replace the lost fluids.

What to eat after your run:
Plan to eat a small snack of protein and carbs within the first hour after running. The carbs replenish glycogen (energy) stores and the protein speeds recovery to your muscles. Once you are beyond the one-hour window your body does not use the nutrients as effectively. A small snack within an hour of running will also prevent becoming so hungry later that you end up bingeing. Choose whole grains, because they have more nutrients and will help you stay full longer. Your post-run snack might include one of these:

- a cheese stick and a handful of whole grain pretzels
- half a peanut butter and jelly sandwich on whole wheat bread
- half a turkey sandwich on whole wheat with hummus instead of mayo
- a premixed recovery drink (about 150 calories)
- 8 ounces of low fat organic chocolate milk (my personal favorite—chocolate milk has the perfect protein to carb ratio!)

Runs over an hour

As your runs increase in mileage, you will most likely find that they last between an hour and three hours depending on your pace. What you eat and when you eat it will greatly impact how you feel on your longer runs.

What to eat before your run:
If you have over an hour before your run, then I recommend a 200–300 calorie meal such as one of these:

- a bowl of oatmeal with handful of fruit
- half of a bagel with two tablespoons peanut butter or a piece of cheese
- an english muffin with jam or peanut butter and a banana
- an 8 ounce fruit smoothie made with yogurt
- an energy bar
- a bowl of cereal with non-fat milk
- an egg on white toast

What to eat during your run:
Your body cannot store enough energy to keep you running strong beyond an hour, so you must ingest fuel during your run. You have to train your digestive system to run a half marathon just like you have to train your heart, lungs and muscles. It's imperative that you practice this during your long runs to determine what works best for you. There is nothing worse than trying a new sports drink or gel on race day only to discover it upsets your stomach and you spend 10 minutes of your race time in the porta-potty!

You will also need to replenish potassium and electrolytes that are lost as you sweat, so drinking water is not enough. You should aim to ingest 100–250 calories of carbs every hour. This can be in the form of a sports drink, such as Gatorade or Powerade. A 16 ounce bottle of Gatorade provides 100 calories.

That probably sounds like a lot to drink in an hour, doesn't it? That's why we need to practice.

Another option is energy gels or chews. These are made up of simple carbs and electrolytes (some have amino acids and vitamins as well) that are made to quickly digest in your stomach. An energy gel or 3–4 chews typically provide 100 calories. They can be found at specialty running stores and many big box sports stores. I suggest buying several different flavors and types until you find one you like and that works for you. Be sure to check the labels, because some have caffeine in them. Caffeine helps speed the digestion process, getting the energy to your muscles faster and delaying the sense of fatigue, but if you are not used to caffeine you may find it upsets your stomach.

Again, your target should be at least one gel or 4 chews an hour—and remember to drink several sips of water with it. Taking a gel without water can upset your stomach. I find that the gels work best for me if I take them before I need them (in other words, before I run out of energy) so I typically take a gel every 45 minutes. That works best for my body, but you will need to determine what works best for yours.

What to eat after your run:
Again, eating a combination of carbs and protein within one hour of running is crucial to replenish your glycogen stores and speed recovery to your tired muscles. Aim for a small meal, such as:

- a peanut butter and jelly sandwich on whole wheat
- a turkey sandwich on whole wheat
- a premixed recovery drink
- an 8 ounce smoothie made with protein powder and fruit
- yogurt with fruit mixed in
- a bowl of whole grain cereal and skim milk
- 8 ounces of low fat, organic chocolate milk

I still have bad runs when I don't take the time to eat properly. There have been days where I've literally run out of gas 17 miles into a 20 mile training run because I didn't eat before I ran, and didn't take in enough fuel during my run. You have made the commitment to train, so don't let that time and training go to waste because you failed to fuel your body properly!

Now let's spend a few minutes discussing a rather uncomfortable subject: upset stomachs while running. Upset stomachs can put a huge cramp (literally!) on your run, causing you to detour to the nearest bathroom. It's wise to give yourself enough time for your stomach to digest its content before you start, which is why I suggest at least an hour between when you eat and when you begin running. That gives your body time to process it, and send you to the bathroom.

Some find that drinking a cup of coffee before a morning run helps this process. If you find that you suffer from an upset stomach while running, avoid fiber and whole grains for several hours before your run since those foods digest more slowly. Sometimes choosing plain bagels, bananas, white pita or oatmeal instead of whole wheat breads can help relieve nausea and stomach distress. Again, everyone's bodies react differently so it may take some experimenting before you discover what works best for you. That's why it's important to start now, early in your training.

As you experiment with what foods work best before, during, and after your runs, write them down in your training log. You may find that a certain combination of food, gels, and water give you the perfect amount of energy! If you find you simply can't eat before your run without stomach issues, you'll need to make sure you eat plenty the night before (or if running at night, eat plenty at lunch). Then concentrate on training your stomach during exercise—slowly increasing your carb intake as your stomach allows. You can train your stomach, it just takes a little patience and diligence.

Hydration

The simplest way to tell if you are adequately hydrating is to regularly check the color and quantity of your urine.[14] When your urine is pale yellow and plentiful you are probably properly hydrated. (If you take vitamin supplements your urine color may be darker, so you'll need to judge your hydration by volume).

Proper fluid intake varies between individuals and many factors come into play, so there isn't a "one size fits all" formula for how much you should drink each day. A good rule of thumb is eight glasses of non-alcoholic liquid per day. Those who exercise 30–60 minutes, 3–4 times a week will probably maintain a proper water balance just through normal eating and drinking.[15] If you exercise intensely or sweat excessively, you'll need to replenish the fluid you lose through sweat as well. Again, the color and quantity of your urine can help you determine if you are drinking enough.

Symptoms that you are dehydrated include: muscle cramps, nausea, vomiting, dizziness, confusion, disorientation, weakness, inability to concentrate, and irrational behavior.[16] Dehydration is cumulative, so if you begin to feel chronically fatigued and headachy, it may be a sign you need to drink more fluids.

Although it doesn't usually happen in a half marathon, sometimes runners can drink too much water during a run, causing a condition known as hyponatremia. Hyponatremia occurs when blood sodium is diluted to abnormally low levels. Symptoms of hyponatremia are similar to dehydration, sometimes making it difficult to diagnose: fatigue, disorientation, bloating, swelling of hands and feet, confusion, and headache.[17] A good way to avoid hyponatremia is to drink sports drinks and not just water during your runs, as well as drinking small amounts regularly rather than gulping down a huge amount of water once or twice a day.

The best way to maintain proper fluid levels for our training is to:

- sip fluids, all day long,
- drink 8–10 ounces of water an hour before you exercise,
- drink a total of 8–16 ounces of sports drink during exercise that last over an hour,
- drink 8 ounces of water after you exercise, and
- keep an eye on your urine—it should be pale yellow and plentiful.

Enjoy your recovery training week! Next week we are going to step up our mileage and learn about the importance of running form. Keep up the hard work!

Week 5

Proper Form

After completing this week's training and homework, you will:

- know how to determine your cadence,
- have the tools and exercises to improve your running form,
- know how to practice Paul's instructions for peace, and
- understand physical and spiritual imbalances.

> *"Walk with me and work with me—watch how I do it. Learn the unforced rhythms of grace. I won't lay anything heavy or ill-fitting on you. Keep company with me and you'll learn to live freely and lightly."*
> Matthew 11:28-30 (MSG)

Welcome to Month 2 of this program. I wish I were there with you to give you a great big high-five for making it this far. I am so proud of you!

After a nice week of recovery runs, get ready to step up your training this week! I always love training after I have had a little bit of recovery. My body and mind feel strong and ready to go. You will most likely be running for over an hour on your long run this week. Look back at your training log from two weeks ago, when you ran seven miles. If it was a tough run for you, see if there is anything you can do differently this time to make it easier. If it was a great run, see what you can duplicate to have another great one! Don't forget to pay attention to what you eat before and after your runs. Proper hydration and nutrition will make your long run much more enjoyable and your recovery quicker.

If you take a look at your training schedule for this week, you will see that workout one has a range from 40–50 minutes. From now on some of your mid-week runs (and runs/walks, if you are following the run/walk program) will have a range of times. If your training is going well and you feel your body can handle an extra few minutes of running, aim for the upper minutes. However, if you do not feel ready to add additional minutes to your run then run for the lowest amount of minutes in the range. Each week you will have the opportunity to choose within the range, according to how you feel that day. You will be prepared for your half marathon as long as you complete at least the minimum time each day. If you find you are struggling to finish your long runs, this week may be a perfect week to transition to the run/walk program, located in Appendix F. Sometimes all your body needs to finish is a few calculated breaks, which can be easily accomplished by using a consistent run/walk ratio. If you find you can run for some of the shorter, mid-week runs, but need to transition to a run/walk ratio for your longer runs, that is fine. Again, the goal is finishing strong—it doesn't matter if walking is part of that finish!

I also hope you are including some core exercises in your weekly routine. It is just as important to strengthen your core as it is to complete your mileage. Because I love to run, sometimes I neglect this since I'd rather run an extra half hour than do my core exercises. But I won't be the strongest runner I can be if all I do is run. I have to spend time on my core. So make sure you are devoting half an hour a couple of times a week to strengthening your core.

Wow, we have covered an awful lot so far! I hope you are beginning to see the relationship between our bodies, spirits, and minds. It never ceases to amaze me how God continues to use my physical training to show me His plan for our spiritual lives. I am thankful every day for His revelations.

Week 5 TRAINING SCHEDULE

There are 5 workouts (4 runs, 1 cross training) and 2 rest days each week.
The workout days are flexible, however use 1 rest day after your longest run.

WEEK 5	WORKOUT 1	WORKOUT 2	WORKOUT 3	WORKOUT 4	WORKOUT 5	WORKOUT 6	WORKOUT 7
PLAN	Easy Run 40-50 min	X-train 30 min + 20 min core	Easy Run 35 min (spend 10 min on form)	(before running, do 5 min of form exercises) **Easy Run** 45 min + 10 min core	Rest	Long Run 8 miles (concentrate on form for 2 miles)	Rest
LOG							

Always spend 5-10 minutes warming up and 5-10 minutes cooling down. This can be included in your total time/mileage.

Long Run: These should be at an easy, conversational pace.
Easy Run: Easy runs should be at an easy, conversational pace. On a scale of 1-10 (10 being all out effort), an easy run should feel like a 5-6.
X-train: Cross-training. Anything other than running, such as swimming, biking, walking, strength training.
LOG: This is where you write what you ACTUALLY did that day, along with a description of how you prepared and how you felt.
Core: Choose a few core exercises and spend time strengthening your core after your run.
Form: Concentrate on your running form during your run. Arms, neck, foot placement, breathing...
Form Exercises: Butt kicks and high knees.

"Walk with me and work with me — watch how I do it. Learn the unforced rhythms of grace. I won't lay anything heavy or ill-fitting on you. Keep company with me and you'll learn to live freely and lightly." — MATTHEW 11:28-30 (MSG)

(This page is left blank so that you can cut out the workout plan on the other side and display it where you'll see it regularly.)

Study Day One

This week brings us to the topic of proper running form. When I first started running, I didn't pay much attention to my running form. I had the misconception that because I had been running since I was a toddler, I knew what I was doing. Unlike golf or tennis or skiing, where learning proper form was imperative to the sport, I figured as long as I put one foot in front of the other that was good enough.

That may be true if I was simply going to play a game of tag with my kids for a few minutes, but training for races requires me to run for over an hour several times a week. Improving my form helps me become more efficient and makes my body less prone to injury. Improved form can reduce the shock—which is as much as five times your body weight—that travels up my body with each step I take.[1] Rather than allowing the parts of my body to work against each other, I can train my arms, legs, hips, and core to work together in harmony, providing an effortless, injury-free run.

I learned the importance of proper running form the hard way—after nursing a chronically sore knee, and being unable to improve my speed no matter what I tried. I met with a running coach who watched my technique and gave me some pointers. That, coupled with a little bit of research on proper form, made all the difference for me. Although I'm unable to personally analyze your running technique here, there are some general things you can do to improve your form and make your runs less stressful on your body.

Cadence (or stride rate) and foot strike

Cadence is the average number of steps you take per minute when you run. Your cadence will improve your pace and your running efficiency. Elite runners typically have a stride rate of about 180 steps per minute—90 steps on each foot. Most average runners have a cadence well below this, which means their steps are too large and they are likely to overstride.

Overstriding is when you land heel first, with your foot in front of you rather than underneath your body. Overstriding is detrimental for a couple of reasons. First, it slows you down. Each time your heel hits the ground your momentum is decreased. Essentially you are braking with every step you take! Once I learned to take smaller steps, my pace improved dramatically—without me having to use more energy.

Second, overstriding creates a larger shock impact to your body with each step. Landing on your heel means you have straightened your knee. This doubles the shock that reverberates up your ankles, knees, hips, and back.[2] Shortening your stride helps you land on your mid-foot or even your forefoot (the pad of your foot, almost on your toes) with a soft knee, right under your center of gravity, which lessens the impact.

This week during a mid-week run your job is to determine what your cadence is. You can do this by counting how many times your right foot hits the ground in one minute, then multiply that number by two to determine your cadence.

Here are three exercises that can help you improve your cadence and foot placement.

Butt Kicks: Keeping your knees in place, kick your feet up until you kick yourself in your behind (heel to glute). Be sure to swing your arms at the same time. You can do this in place or move forward with each kick. Do three sets of 30 seconds each.

High Knees: As you run, lift your knees high. Don't kick out your feet; just lift your knees high—running in place. This exercise engages your hip flexors which are seldom used, so to avoid pulling one, just start with a few high knees and work your way up to three sets of 30 seconds each.[3]

Strides: Near the end of a run, run an easy sprint (about 70-80 percent of your maximum pace) for 30 seconds, concentrating on quick foot turn over. Think fast, but relaxed. Do not run so fast that you can't maintain good running form. Rest for 30 seconds to a minute and repeat the stride. Work up to 8-10 strides near the end of every run.

Another way to improve your cadence is simply to increase your foot turn over by one or two steps in the middle of a run. If your current cadence is 160 steps per minute, spend a few minutes running at a cadence of 162 steps. As you shorten your stride, keep your knees flexed and land softly on your mid-foot or forefoot. You should not be able to hear your foot hit the ground. If you hear your foot thud onto the ground with each step, you are not landing softly.

You will find that your cadence will stay nearly the same, regardless of your pace. In other words, whether you are running an 8-minute mile or a 12-minute mile, your steps per minute should be about the same. Improving your cadence and foot strike isn't something you can change overnight; it takes time and diligent practice. It took me months before my mid-foot strike began to feel normal. To this day, I still practice improving my cadence and foot strike, or I find that I revert back to my old habits.

Core and hips

As you run, you want a strong, solid core that you engage with each step. Here is where those core exercises will pay off! Your bottom should be underneath, not behind you. The power to swing each leg does not come from your quads or hamstrings; it comes from your hips and core.

Resist the urge to cave in your abdomen as you tire. Some coaches believe that you should lean slightly forward at the chest, without bending at the waist, as though you are falling forward. However, if that posture compromises your strong core, then I would rather you stay upright to take advantage of your core strength.

Arm swing

Good form doesn't end with your legs; proper arm swing is just as important as proper foot placement. You waste a lot of energy with sloppy arm swings. A proper arm swing has the arms bent 90 degrees at the elbow, swinging like pendulums from the shoulders. Rather than your arms crossing in front of your chest (which causes your body to twist from side to side), they should move parallel to your body with elbows close to your side. Imagine that your elbows are scraping the ground with each swing.[4]

I find that it helps when I turn my wrists up and my thumbs out, away from my body as though I am holding something in the palm of my hands. Your elbows naturally stay close to your sides when you twist your wrists up. Your hands should be loose and relaxed as you swing your arms from your shoulders, not wasting energy on clenched fists.

Keeping your elbows close to your side will also help your feet and ankles stay in alignment. If your elbows kick out like chicken wings, so will your feet. And believe it or not, your arms dictate your pace. The faster you swing your arms, the faster your feet move!

Head, shoulders, and chest

Your head should stay relatively still as you run. If your head is moving up and down a lot with each step, you're wasting energy. All of your power should be focused on forward movement, not up and down motion. Your shoulders should be relaxed, not hunched up to your chin or curved forward into your chest. Keep your chest open and strong as you tire, resisting the urge to cave in.

Breathing

Even something as natural as breathing can make or break a run. Beginning runners have a tendency to inhale through their noses and exhale through their mouths, severely limiting the amount of oxygen delivered to the lungs. Instead, inhale and exhale through both the nose and mouth, using your diaphragm. If you're breathing properly, your chest won't move! Your stomach should move in and out with each breath. (After a long, hard race my diaphragm will actually ache from use!) Many elite runners breathe in a 2:2 pattern—every two steps they breathe in or out. I personally breathe in a 3:2 pattern. I inhale deeply for three steps and exhale deeply for 2 steps. As someone who gets side stitches occasionally, I find it helps to not inhale on the same foot each time. (If you suffer from exercise-induced asthma, inhaling through your mouth may aggravate it. You may want to stick with inhaling through your nose, which moistens and warms the air before it hits your lungs.)[5]

I find that as I tire, my form can get sloppy; but it's when I tire, that good form is most important, and good form keeps me fresher longer! To help me maintain good form throughout my run, I do a "body check" every few minutes. I start at my feet and move up my body, making sure that each part of my body has proper form. I shake out my arms, shoulders, and neck, making sure I'm relaxed.

I realize that is a lot of information to try to put into action. Again, I can't stress enough that learning proper running form takes time and practice. Spend a few minutes during each run concentrating on your form: arm placement, foot placement, strong core, cadence, and breathing. The more you practice, the more natural it will feel! I still have to remind myself to flip my wrists up and keep my elbows near my side; this is not a natural arm swing for me. I also have to remind myself to land on my mid-foot as I tire.

But, overall, the practice has paid off for me. I find my runs are smoother and more enjoyable as my body parts work together. A good word would be *peaceful*. Even though I am working hard and running strong, there is a sense of calmness, of peace, to my body when I am in good form. All my body parts are fitting together, doing their jobs in harmony. Running is less stressful when you use good form!

If I had to define proper spiritual form, I would sum it up in three words: *Walk with Jesus*. His life and message teach us to walk spiritually in proper form. In *The Message*, Eugene Peterson paraphrases Jesus' words in Matthew 11:28-30 as, *"Walk with me and work with me—watch how I do it. Learn the unforced rhythms of grace. I won't lay anything heavy or ill-fitting on you. Keep company with me and you'll learn to live freely and lightly."* In other words, if we walk with Jesus and follow His example, we will learn how to live with less effort, with a natural rhythm.

According to your Bible version, what does Jesus say in Matthew 11:28-30?

_____

_____

_____

_____

I once had a friend who seemed to thrive on chaos. Everything in her life was a crisis, and her demeanor was frenetic. Just being around her stressed me out—it was like being in the middle of a tornado!

Most of her "crises" were self-inflicted because she was always worked up into a frenzy. Although she had a relationship with Jesus, she hadn't yet internalized His "unforced rhythms of grace." There was no rest in her soul or her body, just wasted energy and chaos.

I have also known people who have an air of grace; who seem to effortlessly walk through life's trials. I know their lives are not trouble free—in fact, some of them have suffered more than I ever care to in my lifetime. Yet there is a sense of peace and calmness about them. They have found that rhythm of life that Jesus offers all of us.

When you are walking through a tough situation, do you typically work yourself into a frenzy, worrying about the outcome and attempting to control the situation; or do you give that situation over to God through prayer and through His word?

_____

_____

I personally fall somewhere in the middle of those two extremes. While I may not live in the midst of self-induced chaos, I do struggle at times to live within Jesus' peaceful rhythm. However, I know that Jesus promises me that peace, if I continue to walk with Him.

Read Psalm 119:165. What does the psalmist say about peace?

_____

The Hebrew word *shalowm* in this verse can be translated as *completeness, soundness, welfare, peace:*
> —*safety, soundness (in body)*
> —*welfare, health, prosperity*
> —*peace, quiet, tranquility, contentment*[6]

When we love God and walk in His ways we find peace. Now flip to Isaiah 26:3. What does the prophet say about peace in this verse?

_____

_____

This verse doesn't say that our lives will be trouble free, but if we fix our thoughts on God, we don't have to be shaken by the surrounding chaos. In fact, in both the Old and New Testament, God's Word says that creating peace requires work. Look up Psalm 34:14 and 1 Peter 3:11. What do both of these verses say about peace?

_____

Just like learning to run with my elbows at my side while landing on my mid-foot requires conscious effort, creating a life of peace, whether in relationships, or within yourself requires work. Paul actually gives us instructions on how to achieve that proper spiritual form in Philippians 4:6-9. Let's go verse by verse in the NIV and write down these instructions:

Do not be _____ about anything, but in every situation, by _____ and _____, with _____, present your requests to God. And the _____, which transcends all understanding, will guard your hearts and your minds in Christ Jesus. Finally, brothers and sisters, whatever is _____, whatever is _____, whatever is _____, whatever is _____, whatever is _____, whatever is _____—if anything is excellent or _____—think about such things. Whatever you have learned or received or heard from me, or seen in me—_____. And the God of peace _____.

The key to living in God's peace is to turn our worries over to Him with a grateful heart. Rather than wasting our energy on all the bad things that could happen, we can and should fill our days with prayer and our minds with what is praiseworthy.

That's easier said than done for some of us, right? That's why Paul says we have to practice! It doesn't feel natural to give our troubles to God any more than it feels natural to run with a cadence of 180 steps per minute!

How do we practice this? Every time you begin to worry, practice turning that worry into prayer. Practice being grateful for all that God has given you. Practice finding the good in all people, and in all situations.

As I have begun to practice Paul's instructions in my own life, I have experienced that peace that God promises. Do I still worry occasionally? Of course. Do I sometimes have a grumpy heart rather than a grateful heart? Unfortunately, yes. I am a work in progress; but God has proven to me if I continue to seek Him and walk with Him, I can learn how to live freely and lightly.

Jesus' life was a testimony to having a peace that passes human under-standing—right down to His death. He doesn't promise that our race will always be easy and that we won't at times be weary. After all, His own life was fraught with conflict and pain! But He does tell us that if we take our burdens to Him with a thankful heart, He will give us rest.

This week, turn off your music as you run. Listen to your breathing. Count your steps. Become aware of your elbows and arms, shoulders, and core. Take some time to teach your body to work towards a running form that is less stressful and more peaceful.

Study Day Two

> *"My grace is all you need. My power works best in weakness."*
> 2 Corinthians 12:9

One of the things I love about God is that His Word is consistent. As I finished typing our Day One lesson for this week, the monthly e-mail newsletter from my church in Florida hit my inbox. In it my pastor wrote, "A life of gratitude is a life of peace." Don't you love it when God puts something on your heart through His word, and then everything around you confirms it? It's as though God is saying, "You're on the right track!" I find that very encouraging.

I hope you had an opportunity to count your cadence. If you did, write it here: _____. In a few weeks we are going to recount our cadence to see if we have made improvements, so keep at those exercises!

During your runs this week, did you take time to notice your arms and feet? What did you discover about your form?

_____

_____

_____

_____

Don't worry if you discovered you have chicken elbows, are a noisy heel striker, and breathe only through your nose. As Beth Moore says, "Awareness is always the first step to freedom."[7] Over time, a more efficient, less stressful running form will feel natural—if you continue to practice it!

Let's take a minute to review the instructions Paul gave us to help us live more freely and lightly. (Turn to Philippians 4:6-9 for help.)

_____

_____

_____

_____

Did a situation arise this week that allowed you to practice these instructions?

_____

_____

_____

Today, I want to delve more deeply into our physical and spiritual form. Lace up those running shoes because today we are gonna' run hard!

Sometimes we have barriers that keep us from being able to truly experience proper spiritual form—a form that leads to peace in our lives. Let's start by first looking at physical compensations that can inhibit us from running with proper form.

As a personal trainer, part of my job is to determine if my clients have any muscle imbalances that need to be addressed before beginning a strength-training routine. A simple definition of **muscle imbalance** is when one muscle (or group of muscles) is weak, causing the opposite muscle (or group of muscles) to compensate and become stronger. There are many reasons we might have muscle imbalances: past trauma, lack of core strength, repetitive movement, poor training technique, emotional duress, and poor posture are a few.[8]

Poor posture is one of the most common causes of muscle imbalance. When we spend most of our day sitting at desks, in our cars, and on the couch, our hip flexors (the muscles in the front of our hips) become tight and shortened. Tight hip flexors create a forward tilt in our pelvis. A tilt in our pelvis causes our hamstrings (the muscles in the back of our thighs) to stretch and weaken.[9]

If muscle imbalances are left untreated, new inappropriate movement patterns are established. These movement patterns (such as an arched lower back or rounded shoulders) become our new "normal." Eventually these new movement patterns will cause chronic pain as muscles, joints, and tendons move in ways they were never created to move.

Now, let's say we want to begin a running program. Running is a repetitive movement that involves our hamstring muscles. If we don't address our weak, stretched hamstrings, we will most likely strain them. If nothing else, weak hamstrings will cause our quads (the quadriceps are the muscles in the front of our thighs) and other muscles and joints to work harder, causing all manner of other strains and pains!

Have you ever sprained an ankle and then noticed the opposite leg becoming tired and sore? You compensated for the sore ankle by favoring it and putting unusual stress on the other leg, causing a muscle imbalance.

The key is to address the muscle imbalance(s) and implement a stretching and strengthening program—stretching the tight, shortened muscle and strengthening the stretched, weak muscle—that corrects the imbalance and retrains the muscles to work as God intended.

Most of us have one or more muscle imbalances in our bodies. I can't identify and address your individual muscle imbalances through the pages of this book, but the stretching and core exercises I've included are a good place to start—as long as you are not experiencing any chronic pain. The exercises in Appendices B and C will help your entire body become stronger and more flexible, which can prevent muscle imbalances. If you find that you are continually battling pain, I recommend that you find a good personal trainer or physical therapist. They can diagnose any imbalances and create a treatment program to get all of your muscles working to the best of their ability.

Just as a weakened muscle causes another muscle to compensate, we have a tendency to compensate for our "spiritual imbalances." A spiritual imbalance is an area of weakness in our lives. Perhaps we have grown so accustomed to compensating for it that we don't even know this weakness exists. Whatever the weakness may be, it is a barrier to that peace that God offers us. It hinders us from being fully available to God.

For example, imagine that you struggle with insecurity. Ever since you can remember, you have felt inadequate. You struggle to fit in, but never really feel like you belong anywhere. To compensate for your feelings of insecurity, you become critical and judgmental of those around you: *I can't be friends with her—she dresses funny* may sound silly, but it's the type of thing we often come up with to mask our own issues. Or, *He's too friendly; he must have an ulterior motive.* You come across as snobbish and aloof because you are now in the habit of judging others to compensate for your insecurities. Your feelings of security, of belonging, are your weakened spiritual muscle. Your judgmental spirit is the muscle that takes over. It's hard to find God's peace when you have a strong spirit of judgment controlling you.

Go back up to the list of causes for muscle imbalances and write them here:

_____   _____

_____   _____

_____   _____

Now look at those causes in the light of all we have discussed about our spiritual training over the last five weeks. Circle any that could be attributed to spiritual imbalances.

I think we can circle all six! Let's look at those causes for a minute:

- **Past trauma.** Emotional trauma, if not dealt with, can certainly hinder proper spiritual form.
- **Weak core.** As we discussed in earlier weeks, not having a strong spiritual core can lead to many kinds of weakness.

- **Repetitive movement.** Doing the same thing over and over can lead to spiritual imbalance. God wants us to grow and change!
- **Poor training technique.** If we are not consistently in the Word (our training program) and spending time each day with God in prayer and/ or meditation, we will most likely end up with a spiritual imbalance.
- **Emotional duress.** I think it is easy to see the relationship between emotional duress (which could manifest as anxiety, depression, obsessiveness, just to name a few) and our spiritual imbalance. You might have been surprised, though, that emotional duress also causes muscle imbalance. The amount of stress you are under and your emotional well-being can cause physical issues. There is a direct link between our emotional well-being and our physical well-being!
- **Poor posture.** I bet you are wondering how I'm going to relate that to spiritual weakness! To me, proper spiritual posture is being humble, acknowledging that God is God, and you are not; being aware that He is worthy to be praised, and giving Him His rightful place in your life. Both James 4:10 and 1 Peter 5:6 speak of a posture of humbleness before the Lord. If I had to visualize proper spiritual poster, it would be me, down on my knees, praising the One who created the universe and is in control of everything. The minute we start thinking too highly of ourselves and not highly enough of God, we have become spiritually imbalanced!

Let's see how this all fits together. During my childhood, a couple of traumatic experiences caused me to feel like my life was out of control. I didn't know the Lord at that time, so I didn't know that what was happening was in His control and that I could rely on Him for my strength.

Instead, feeling out of control led to an eating disorder. If I could control nothing else, at least I could control what I ate (or in my case, didn't eat). Pangs of hunger and obsessive thoughts about food became my idols.

Talk about a spiritual *and* physical imbalance! Even after I came to know the Lord, every time I felt out of control I compensated by not eating. God offered me healing and the revelation that in order to gain control of my life, I needed to give the control to Him. Although I am fully healed, I realize that the tendency to use food as control still exists within me; but I take comfort in 2 Corinthians 12:9's words that His power is made perfect in my weaknesses.

Sometimes God uses our weakness to remind us to rely on Him for our strength. Paul had a "thorn in [his] flesh" (2 Corinthians 12:7) to keep him from becoming proud. Paul doesn't tell us if this thorn was physical or mental, but he does tell us that he prayed for God to take it away, and God's reply was "My grace is all you need. My power works best in weakness" (2 Corinthians 12:9). Paul chose to embrace his weakness, not mask it or ignore it, knowing that when he was weak, Christ's power in him was strong. God was Paul's spiritual balance.

My childhood traumas caused me to feel out of control and I compensated by taking control of food, creating a spiritual imbalance that kept me from fully experiencing a relationship with my Lord. Spiritual imbalances can take many forms, and the ways we compensate are just as varied. For example…

- *When we are unable to trust, we compensate by becoming controlling.*
- *When we are discontent, we compensate with envy.*
- *When we lack compassion, we have a spirit of indifference.*

There are entire Bible studies devoted to the different ways we compensate for our spiritual weaknesses (written by men and women who are much smarter than me), so I don't pretend to be all-inclusive here. Take a few minutes to think about a spiritual imbalance you may have in your own life. You may need to pray for God's help in revealing it to you. Write down your weakness and how you think you compensate for it.

_____

_____

_____

_____

If you have not yet allowed God to heal you, know that He wants nothing more than to make you whole! Invite Him into your weakness. It is only through Him that we can be made strong. Our security, self-esteem, contentment, love, and compassion all come from Him. The spiritual compensations we use to make us feel strong only hinder us from a experiencing a full relationship with Him. We will never experience that true peace, and be able to walk with Him lightly and freely if we don't allow God to take our burdens and place His yoke upon us (Matthew 11:28-30).

Thank you for the privilege of joining you on this journey. I am humbled by your commitment. I know this may have been a tough lesson for some of you, and I am proud of you for persevering.

Week 6

Matters of the Heart

After completing this week's training and homework, you will:

- understand the purpose of different heart rate tests,
- know how to test different heart rates,
- describe the different conditions of our spiritual hearts, and
- know the steps to a healthy spiritual heart.

> *"Guard your heart, for everything you do flows from it."*
> Proverbs 4:23 (TNIV)

I can hardly believe we are halfway through this program! As excited as I am for our half-marathon, I am sad to think about this all being over. I hope you have found the first half to be fun, uplifting, and thought-provoking. Let's spend the second half of our training committed to really digging in, and praying that we hear God's heart for each of us.

Now is the time to do a little research about the race you plan to run. Most races have a Web site loaded with information. You need to find out:

When does your race start?
If your race has a 6:00 a.m. start, but you usually run in the evening, your body will not be used to an early morning run. There is a big difference between

running first thing in the morning and later in the day. For example, your nutritional needs will be different in the morning. After an entire night of fasting, you need to eat some carbs and protein that will not upset your stomach. (Go back and look at my suggestions in Week 4 for quick-digesting carbs.) While it isn't necessary to run all of your training runs at the time of your race, practicing a few runs during those hours will prepare you for race day.

What is the race terrain?

Is your race hilly? Are the hills located near the beginning when you're fresh, or toward the end when you're tired? Do you run over any bridges or up any interstate ramps? (Believe it or not, bridges and interstate ramps are deceptively tough—especially in the last miles of the race.) Are you mostly on streets, sidewalks, or biking trails? For instance, the course for the "26.2 With Donna" race in Jacksonville has several miles of running on the beach (the packed sand near the water), and the last mile is uphill over a highway overpass. While you may not be able to practice running on the beach, it at least helps to know when to expect it. The Disney World marathons include several interstate on and off ramps and a lot of highway running, as well as at least a mile on a wooden boardwalk.

Most race Web sites have a course map and an elevation change map so you can see where the hills are. Now is the time to try to recreate the race terrain in your runs, as much as possible. If your race has a hill in the last miles, try to finish your long runs with a hill. If your race has bridges, see if you can find a bridge to run over during your long runs. The more prepared you are for race day terrain, the better race you will have!

Knowing the course ahead of time will also help you decide what goals you will have for the race. Trying to set a Personal Record (that is, trying to run your fastest time for that distance) will be much tougher if the route is very hilly or has a section of cobblestone streets. In fact, if I know my goal is to set a PR, I choose a race course that I know will help me run fast (i.e. a

Week 6 TRAINING SCHEDULE

There are 5 workouts (4 runs, 1 cross training) and 2 rest days each week.
The workout days are flexible, however use 1 rest day after your longest run.

WEEK 6	WORKOUT 1	WORKOUT 2	WORKOUT 3	WORKOUT 4	WORKOUT 5	WORKOUT 6	WORKOUT 7
PLAN	Easy Run 40-50 min *(spend 10 min on form)*	X-train 30 min + 20 min core	Easy Run 35 min OR Easy Pace 10 Hard Pace 15 Easy Pace 10	Easy Run 45-55 min + 10 min core	Rest *(find Delta HR today)*	Long Run 9 miles *(in mile 8, do 5 strides, 30 sec each)*	Rest
LOG							

Always spend 5-10 minutes warming up and 5-10 minutes cooling down. This can be included in your total time/mileage.

Long Run: These should be at an easy, conversational pace.
Easy Run: Easy runs should be at an easy, conversational pace. On a scale of 1-10 (10 being all out effort), an easy run should feel like a 5-6.
X-train: Cross-training. Anything other than running, such as swimming, biking, walking, strength training.
LOG: This is where you write what you ACTUALLY did that day, along with a description of how you prepared and how you felt.
Core: Choose a few core exercises and spend time strengthening your core after your run.
Form: Concentrate on your running form during your run. Arms, neck, foot placement, breathing...
Delta HR: See page 107 for explanation of Delta Heart Rate exercise.
Strides: 30-second easy sprints, keeping good form, concentrating on quick foot turnover. Allow heart rate to lower in between each stride.

Guard your heart, for everything you do flows from it. — PROVERBS 4:23 (TNIV)

(This page is left blank so that you can cut out the workout plan on the other side and display it where you'll see it regularly.)

smaller race with a flat course). We will talk more about race day goal-setting toward the end of the study, but knowing the course terrain will definitely be a factor in your goals.

What is offered at the water/aid stations?

Most race sites will list what types of liquids and nutritional supplements will be available and at which miles. If you are used to drinking Gatorade on your long runs, but the race provides Powerade, you may want practice with Powerade a few times to make sure your tummy can handle it. I know from unfortunate experience that there's nothing worse than finding out three miles into your race that your stomach can't handle the sports drink the race offers. I once ran a half marathon and discovered the drink being offered was one with protein. I was so surprised by the taste, I almost threw up! It would have been smart of me to have tried the drink out a few times during my long runs. Then, if I decided I really couldn't handle it, I could have carried my own sports drink during the race. I don't necessarily like to carry my own drink during a race, but it would have been a better option for me than a drink I couldn't swallow!

If possible, find out what gel brands will be offered, and when. If you use Powerade gels, but the race is supplying Cliff Shots, you will want to practice with Cliff products. You probably will not be able to find out which flavors will be offered. The gels are usually donated and the flavors are either their standards (such as vanilla, chocolate, or orange) or those that did not sell well (think apple-pie cinnamon). If you can only tolerate one flavor, it is best to just carry your own gels during the race. I can't stand the fruit-flavored gels. Especially after running hard for several miles, the wrong flavor makes me want to throw up. So just in case that's all that's offered, I bring my own gels. That way I have the right amount and can take them when I need them, rather than having to wait until the mile they are offered.

If your race does not have a Web site, it will have a race director (the person responsible for making sure the race goes smoothly). You should be able to send the race director an e-mail with your requests, and someone from the staff should get back to you.

Below, make appropriate notes about your race to help you prepare:

Time of race: _____

Terrain: _____

_____

_____

_____

Hydration/gels: _____

_____

_____

I hope you are making an effort to practice your form on a regular basis. Have you noticed any differences in your running since you have started paying attention to your form? (Faster pace, sore muscles you didn't know existed...)

_____

_____

The first few times I changed my arm swing I found that my chest, back, and shoulder muscles were a little sore. They were not used to being used that much while running!

Changing my foot placement made my shins a little sore, too. If you find that you are so sore you can't run without altering your gait, back off! Take your time implementing better form into your running. You don't have to try to change everything at once.

Take a look at your training schedule this week. If you feel ready, we're going to add a tougher run this week. Read the questions below to determine if you're ready to take on a tougher training schedule and put "yes" or "no" beside each one:

_____ You feel recovered between runs (you're not sore).

_____ You are easily hitting your mileage each week.

_____ You feel like you could run further after each run (even your long runs).

If you answered yes to all three, you're ready to step it up! If you answered yes to two, you may try a tougher schedule; but pay close attention to how you feel and be prepared to step it back down. If you said no to two or more, you best bet is to continue to run each training run at an easy pace. Don't be discouraged! Your goal is to finish your race, not to worry about your pace.

Study Day One

This week we are going to take things to heart! We're going to take a look at how our hearts impact our physical and spiritual health.

Our heart is a muscle about the size of our fist. This little muscle has the all important job of pumping blood through our body, delivering oxygen and nutrients to all of our organs and tissue, and picking up the waste product from our organs and tissue.[1]

Like all muscles, your heart requires exercise to function properly or it will weaken. A weak heart muscle can't pump blood as effectively through your body, forcing it to work harder—which can eventually lead to a heart attack. A few years ago I attended a Heart Zones training seminar. Founded by Sally

Edwards, a former professional triathlete and runner, Heart Zones teaches you to utilize your heart rate while exercising. Through this program, I learned the value of using heart rate as a tool for my fitness training. Your heart rate is the amount of times your heart beats per minute. Monitoring your heart rate can help maintain a healthy, strong heart and body.

The most accurate way to keep track of your heart rate is with a heart rate monitor. There are many different types; the best are those with a watch and a separate chest strap. A good heart rate monitor doesn't have to be expensive. Usually the difference in price has to do with added features, not the heart rate monitor itself.

If you don't have a heart rate monitor, you can determine your heart rate by placing two fingers (not your thumb) on your opposite wrist, below the thumb until you can feel your pulse. Count the times your heart beats for 60 seconds. This method is not as reliable as using a monitor (you usually miss a few beats) so it is important to do each test a few times over several days and determine an average for a more accurate picture of your heart rate. A common shortcut is to count the number of beats for ten seconds and multiply by six, but this has an even higher error rate. I monitor my heart rate (using a heart rate monitor that is linked to my stop watch) on a regular basis to help me determine my fitness level and my ability to recover from my training.

Let's go over a few heart rate definitions and tests that I have found helpful in my training:

Resting heart rate
Your **resting heart rate** is the number of times your heart beats per minutes while your body is at rest. A normal resting heart rate is somewhere between 70-100 beats per minute, depending on the individual. The ideal way to measure your resting heart rate is to take it first thing in the morning, several mornings in a row (to get an average). If this isn't possible, you can measure

your heart rate after quietly lying still for five minutes. Your heart rate may be a bit elevated depending on what you ate or drank during the day, but it is still accurate enough.

Your resting heart rate should drop as you become more fit, as your heart gets stronger and is able to pump more blood further with each contraction. Therefore, once you have an idea of your resting heart rate, rechecking it every so often helps you monitor your fitness level. If one day your resting heart rate is 10-20 beats higher than usual, that's an indicator that you are tired or stressed out and you need to take a day off of training. After you've checked your current resting heart rate, enter it here: _____. This is the first step in becoming aware of your heart health.

Delta heart rate

Your **delta heart rate** measures how much faster your heart beats when it's preparing for work. Monitoring your delta heart rate is a great way to determine if you are stressed out or overly tired. To determine your delta heart rate, do the following exercise:

1) Lie down for at least two minutes. After two minutes, note the lowest number on your heart rate monitor. (If you are using your wrist, count your pulse for 30 seconds after a minute and a half, and multiply that number by 2.)

2) Now stand up. Your heart rate will spike—wait for it to stabilize. Once it is stabilized, note your heart rate. Subtract your lying down heart rate from your standing heart rate.

Take five minutes right now and measure your delta heart rate, either with a heart rate monitor or using your pulse.

1) Stabilized heart rate after standing _____

2) Lowest heart rate lying down _____

3) Subtract (2) from (1) to get your delta heart rate _____

If the delta is:

0-10: Excellent! You are in great shape!
10-20: Average, but you can still work out as planned.
20-30: You are slightly stressed or tired. Do a light work out or easy run today.
30+: Whoa! You are way stressed out! You need to take the day off!

Circle which category you fall in, above. If you find your delta heart rate is over 20, that indicates you are either stressed out emotionally or physically. It can also indicate that you are about to come down with an illness. Either way, take that into account as you train this week. Better to back off your training than to push through and make yourself sick.

Recovery heart rate
Your **recovery heart rate** measures how quickly your heart rate decreases after exercising. As you become more fit, your recovery heart rate will increase. You really need a monitor for this one because the wrist method isn't sufficiently accurate.

To measure yours, immediately after running (or a workout) check your heart rate and note the top number (usually your heart rate will spike a few beats the minute you stop running, so use the highest number). Stand completely still for 60 seconds, and check your heart rate again. Subtract your peak heart rate from your heart rate after standing still for 60 seconds.

1) Top heart rate immediately after exercise _____

2) Heart rate after 60 seconds of stillness _____

3) Subtract (2) from (1) to get your recovery heart rate _____

If the recovery rate is:

<10: You are working too hard for your fitness level and may need to see a doctor to make sure nothing else is going on.
11-20: Fair
21-30: Average fitness
31-40: Good fitness
>41: Athletic!

Checking your recovery heart rate every so often is a great way to determine if your fitness program is actually keeping you fit! A lower recovery heart rate indicates you are either not working your heart hard enough to improve, or you are working so hard you are actually decreasing in fitness. (This can be one of the signs of overtraining, which I cover in Week 7.) I check my recovery heart rate after a harder run, at least once a month.

Heart rate zones and maximum heart rate
I am sure most of you have heard of training within heart rate zones, which are derived from your **maximum heart rate** (MHR). Your maximum heart rate is the fastest your heart can beat in one minute. Needless to say, actually achieving your maximum heart rate is not healthy! The most commonly accepted way to determine your maximum heart rate is the formula: 220 - (your age) = MHR. This is a very inadequate formula! The truth is that maximum heart rate varies greatly from individual to individual and involves many fac-

tors, including fitness level and genetics. It is inaccurate to assume that all 40-year-olds (or all 20-year-olds) have the same maximum heart rate, or that your maximum heart rate decreases with age. If you're fit, your maximum heart rate should stay about the same even as you age. In fact, that formula has been proven to have an error factor of several beats, either way.

Personally, I have a very high maximum heart rate (my theory is because I'm pretty small), and if I used the above formula I would *never* get a hard enough workout. The most accurate way to determine your maximum heart rate is via a stress test in a supervised medical facility. Since most of us don't have access to this (nor is it really necessary), there are other "sub-max" tests that you can take to get a fairly accurate idea of your maximum heart rate.

For the sake of time, I'm not going to discuss sub-max tests or heart rate zones in depth in this chapter. I find that using a Rating Perceived Exertion (RPE) chart like the one on the next page works very well. In fact, I believe it is imperative to become good at listening to our bodies as we train. Becoming too reliant on technology is never the best choice. There are days I leave all of my technology at home, including my music, and I run according to how my body feels. If I feel good, I run faster; if I am gasping for air, I slow down! I stop when I get tired. In a world of distractions and constantly being bombarded with technology, I cherish these runs.

Using a heart rate monitor and heart rate zones should never take the place of being aware of how your body feels. With that said, a heart rate monitor is a good way to enhance the RPE chart and help you train more specifically.

I think the heart's ability to indicate our emotional and physical fitness is truly amazing. Just by taking the time to determine our normal heart rates with various tests gives us a glimpse into the health of our heart! How cool is that? Through exercise, you have the ability to strengthen your heart, lower your resting heart rate, and track this progress with measurable tests. The heart is truly an amazing organ.

RPE	Conversation takes:	Beginner	Intermedi-ate	Advanced	Athlete
1-2	no effort	warm up	warm up	warm up	warm up
3	just a bit of effort	fat loss	warm up	warm up	warm up
4	a little effort	endurance	fat loss	warm up	warm up
5	some effort	x	fat loss	fat loss	fat loss
6	concentrated effort	x	endurance	fat loss	fat loss
7	a lot of effort	x	x	endurance	endurance
8	almost all your effort	x	x	peak level	endurance
9	maximum effort	x	x	x	peak level
10	no talking possible	x	x	x	peak level

Heart rate tests are a great place to measure how exercise is affecting our hearts, but what about the aspects of our heart that we can't measure with our heart rate?

A couple of years ago I watched an ABC News piece entitled "How Bad Are America's Unhealthiest Meals?" A reporter and her producer decided to see how eating one of the meals on a list of "unhealthiest dishes from popular chain restaurants" would affect their heart health. Before they ate these "gut busting dishes," blood samples and ultrasounds gauging the health of their arteries were taken, deeming them both perfectly healthy. Their meals consisted of fried macaroni and cheese, quesadilla burgers, and deep-dish cookie sundaes—for a total of 6190 calories and 187 grams of saturated fat!

As hard as they tried, neither could finish their three-course meals. They both felt sluggish and tired after eating. Two hours later, they retested their blood. The results were frightening! The producer's blood, which was basically clear before he ate, was now cloudy with fat. The reporter's ultrasound revealed that the large dose of saturated fat had caused a chemical reaction in her system, which narrowed her arteries and in turn, made her heart work more intensely. The effects of this enormous meal lasted six hours in their systems.[2]

While most of us do not sit down to a meal of that size every day, the research proves that our diet directly affects our heart. We may not feel it immediately, but each unhealthy meal negatively affects our hearts. In fact, one doctor equated the heart effects of eating a meal as unhealthy as the reporter ate to smoking a cigarette. Over time, those unhealthy meals add up to clogged and hardened arteries and an overworked, stressed-out heart. In other words: **heart disease**.

Heart disease is "any disorder that affects the heart's ability to function normally," and it can take many forms.[3] Research shows that 80% of heart disease *is preventable with better lifestyle habits.*[4] You read that right—80%. Most of us can prevent heart disease by eating more healthily, exercising regularly, controlling our weight, and not smoking. For most of us, an unhealthy heart is the overflow of our poor lifestyle choices.

Why is it, then, that a mostly preventable disease is the number one cause of death in the United States? I think it's because the effects of our poor lifestyle choices are slow and cumulative. We don't necessarily feel our hearts weakening and our arteries hardening until after the damage has been done. Prevention requires protective action.

Our next lesson will dig into the spiritual aspect of our hearts. Until then, take some time to become aware of your heart rate. If you choose to run a little harder this week, these tests will definitely come in handy to help you avoid training too hard!

Study Day Two

*"Then the evil one comes and snatches away the seed
that was planted in their hearts."*
Matthew 13:23

Our last lesson focused on our physical hearts. We discussed three heart-rate tests that help us keep tabs on our cardiac health, and we touched on heart disease.

What lifestyle risk factors affect heart disease?

_____

_____

What percentage of heart disease is actually preventable with proper lifestyle choices? _____

That figure still blows my mind. How we feed and treat our physical heart is either life-giving or life-stealing. The statistics show that, sadly, most people choose to ignore the proactive steps necessary to protect their physical hearts.

We've seen how our physical lives affect the condition of our physical hearts. But how does the condition of our spiritual lives affect the condition of our spiritual heart?

God has a few things to say about the condition of our hearts...over 700 verses worth! That says to me that this is something He cares about deeply! Let's take a look at the meaning of the word *heart* in both biblical languages Hebrew and Greek.

In Hebrew, "heart" or *leb* translates to:
1) inner man, mind, will, heart, understanding[5]

In Greek, the word "heart" or *kardia* (which is where we get the word *cardiac*) means:

a) that organ in the animal body which is the centre of the circulation of the blood, and hence was regarded as the seat of physical life
b) denotes the centre of all physical and spiritual life[6]

In other words, the Bible makes it clear that our hearts are the center of our physical and spiritual lives. Jesus examines heart conditions and their responses to His message in the Parable of the Four Soils. Read Matthew 13:3-9 and 18-23.

What does the seed represent in this parable? (Matthew 13:19)

_____

_____

What do the different soils represent? _____

_____

_____

_____

Spiritual heart disease 1: The hardened heart

What happens to the seed scattered on the footpath? (Matthew 13:4 and 19)

_____

_____

Some people's hearts are so hardened that Christ's message may be heard, but it's not understood. His message never penetrates their hearts, and the enemy snatches it away before it has a chance to take root. Paul describes this type of person in Ephesians 4:17-19. What do people with hardened hearts live for, according to Paul?

_____

_____

The Babylonians were a people of hardened hearts. Read what God said about them in Isaiah 47: 8 and 10. How did He describe them?

_____

_____

They believed their man-made wisdom and knowledge was all they needed. They sought pleasure and power and worshipped idols they created. They were self-righteous, arrogant, and treated God's people ruthlessly. According to Proverbs 28:14, what happens to those who harden their hearts against God?

_____

_____

Trouble is a mild word for what happened to the Babylonians. Continue reading in Isaiah 47:11-15. What did God say would happen to them?

_____

_____

Pharaoh, in Exodus 5-14, suffered from a hardened heart. When I read about the plagues God sent to Pharaoh and his people—yet Pharaoh still refused to believe in the most powerful God—I am dumbfounded. Pharaoh finally caved when God killed the firstborn son of every Egyptian, including Pharaoh's own child; but even then, he was only allowing the Israelites to leave in hopes of getting God to finally leave him alone, not out of a heart of belief and repentance.

I would like to think if I witnessed the signs and miracles that Pharaoh witnessed, I would instantly repent of my sinful ways and believe with all of my heart, but the truth is that, even today, we often see God's handiwork and dismiss it as coincidence or serendipity, the same way Pharaoh claimed the miracles of God were just tricks and magic. The *Christianity Today* editors write, "It shouldn't take clear evidence of the supernatural, or even the unprobable for us to thank God for what goes right."[7] I don't want to deny God's power and glory in my life so many times that He finally allows me to have a permanently hardened heart like He did Pharaoh. As His child, my ears should be able to hear His voice (John 10:27), and my eyes see his works throughout creation if I keep my heart softened.

Spiritual heart disease 2: The shallow heart

What happens to the seeds scattered in rocky soil? (Matthew 13:5-6 and 20-21)

_____

_____

There are those who embrace the Gospel enthusiastically at first, but never allow it to really sink in and take root in their lives. They look good and smell good, but their hearts are not rooted in God's Word.

A shallow-hearted person is a lot like Facebook. If you're familiar with Facebook, then you know it's basically a whole lot of activity without much substance. Don't get me wrong—Facebook is a great way to keep up with what your best friend from fourth grade's brother's son had for dinner, but there's no relationship, no real connection. People only post what they want you to see. A Facebook profile is a shiny veneer of the real person; and the minute a "friend" (who could be someone you have actually never even met) posts an offhanded comment you find offensive, with the click of a button you can "unfriend" them.

A shallow-hearted person fades the moment their beliefs are challenged, yet God promises that we will face persecution.

What do the following verses say about persecution?

Matthew 5:44 _____

_____

John 15:20 _____

_____

2 Timothy 3:12 _____

_____

As Jesus performed miracles while traveling throughout Israel, his group of followers began to grow. Just imagine how exciting it would have been to follow around this amazing man who had the gift of healing and speaking! He healed the blind! He brought people back from the dead! He miraculously fed the crowds with just a few loaves of bread and a couple of fish! As long as He was healing and providing free food, He had great crowds of students who hung on His every word, following Him wherever He went.

But when Jesus did not live up to their expectations, the crowds began grumbling: *What happened to the powerful, conquering Messiah-King, who would rescue the Jews from the political clutch of the Romans? This "messiah's" stories are difficult to understand. This guy is asking me to think about things in a strange way. I might actually have to put in a little bit of effort to follow Him.*

Some of his teachings are actually offensive. Drink blood? Eat flesh? We're Jewish for crying out loud! (See John 6:25-58.)

"At this point many of his disciples turned away and deserted him" (John 6:66). When it's no longer fun to follow Jesus, when that fuzzy, feel-good aura goes away, when someone questions your faith, those with shallow hearts choose to turn and walk away.

But Jesus promises blessing to those who are persecuted in His name. Matthew 5:11 says "Blessed are you when people insult you and persecute you, and falsely say all kinds of evil against you because of me."

Spiritual heart disease 3: The contaminated heart

What happens to the seeds scattered in thorny soil? (Matthew 13:7 and 22)

_____

_____

Like those seeds scattered in rocky soil, some people gladly accept Christ's message—but soon become distracted by the cares of this world. Although they may believe the Word, there is no fruit in their lives. The thorny weeds of greed, lust, worry, and power overtake Christ's message in their hearts.

The contaminated heart is revealed when we discover that our things are more important to us than Christ in our heart. Read the story of the rich young man in Luke 18:18-23. Although the young man had diligently followed all of the commandments, what kept him from completely giving his heart to Jesus?

_____

_____

Although we may not be called to give up all of our belongings in order to follow Christ, He does require us to put Him above everything else in our lives.

A contaminated heart cares more about creating an earthly lifestyle than eternal life; but the desire to acquire and retain wealth, possessions, and status do not create a spiritually fruitful life.

Jesus gives us another example of a contaminated heart with the story of the rich fool in Luke 12:13-21. What does Jesus say about those who spend their time and energy storing wealth on earth?

_____

_____

Jesus goes on to tell us "wherever your treasure is, there your heart will also be" (Matthew 6:21). Paul describes such a heart in 2 Timothy 3:2-5. What is some of the fruit of a contaminated heart?

_____

_____

_____

_____

_____

How do we make sure we are not allowing the weeds of earthly treasure choke out Christ in our heart? Let's take a look at the final "soil" and see.

Spiritual heart health

What happens to the seed scattered in good soil? (Matthew 13:8 and 23)

_____

_____

_____

When we delight in the Lord and meditate on His word we are like "trees planted along the riverbank, bearing fruit each season" (Psalm 1:3). The fruit that springs forth from our hearts and lives is love, joy, peace, patience, kindness, goodness, faithfulness, gentleness, and self-control (Galatians 5:22).

Now I am going to ask a pretty tough question: Which of these four hearts that Jesus describes most represents yours right now? _____

I find that, at times, the aspects of my spiritual life have differing diseases. I may find that I have a contaminated heart during my quiet time with the Lord, but a shallow heart in my obedience. Are there areas of your life that you would say are suffering from different spiritual heart diseases? _____

_____

_____

My goal is to have a fertile heart for the Lord in all areas of my life. What must we do to ensure our hearts are the good soil that Matthew describes? "Guard your heart, for everything you do flows from it" (Proverbs 4:23).

The word *guard* (*natsar* in Hebrew) means to guard, watch, watch over or keep, to preserve.[8] Just as eating a healthy diet, maintaining a healthy weight, exercising, and not smoking help guard our physical hearts from heart disease, there are preventative measures we can take to guard our spiritual hearts. There are choices we can make to keep our hearts fertile and prevent spiritual heart disease.

Our spiritual diet

Jesus warns us "It is what comes from inside that defiles you. For from within, out of a person's heart, come evil thoughts, sexual immorality, theft, murder, adultery, greed, wickedness, deceit, lustful desires, envy, slander, pride, and foolishness" (Mark 7:20-22).

What we fill our minds with overflows out of our hearts. If we spend our time ingesting spiritual junk food with the books we read, the movies and television we watch, and music we listen to, what do you think the overflow of our heart will be?

———————————————————————————————————

Circle the words in Jesus' verse above that are regularly represented in the media we are exposed to, day in and day out. I think it's fair to say that every single sinful behavior should be circled.

We may think that our hearts are not being affected by the world around us; that we can rise above its influences. Believe me, there is no judgment from me here. I'm speaking to myself as I write this. I can justify my spiritual "junk food" with the best of them! But the Bible is very clear that what we allow into our minds changes our hearts. "A good person produces good things from the treasury of a good heart, and an evil person produces evil things from the treasury of an evil heart. What you say flows from what is in your heart" (Luke 6:45).

Read Deuteronomy 6:5-8 and Psalm 119:11. What is to be on our hearts and minds? ————————————————————————

God's message is evident all around us. He doesn't hide it from us…but He does want it hidden *in* us. "No, the message is very close at hand; it is on your lips and in your heart so that you can obey it" (Deuteronomy 30:14). If our thought-life is filled with His word, then naturally what will flow from our hearts will be from Him.

Our spiritual weight

What words come to your mind if I asked you to describe a heavy heart?

———————————————————————————————————

———————————————————————————————————

Look up the following verses and write down what happens to our hearts and minds under the weight of rebellion.

Isaiah 1:5-6 _____

_____

Jeremiah 5:23-25 _____

_____

Psalm 107:10-12 _____

_____

Rebellious, disobedient, bitter hearts are heavy hearts. Jesus tells us in Luke 21:34 that we are to guard our hearts, being careful not to weigh them down with the cares of this world and the pursuit of earthly pleasure.

What comes to mind when you think of a light heart?

_____

Joy, laughter, contentment, peace, and thankfulness come to my mind when I think of a light heart. Let's look at how a light heart can affect our attitudes, even in the midst of tribulations. How did the prophet Jeremiah describe his heart in Jeremiah 15:16?

_____

_____

Jeremiah uttered these words in the midst of feeling utterly alone, an outcast from society. As God's mouthpiece, it was his duty to tell the people what they did not want to hear; yet God's words sustained him with joy and delight. Oh, if I could only have that attitude in the midst of my suffering!

God wants to lift the burden of a heavy heart from us. When we seek Him with a heart of repentance and praise, He offers us a light heart, even in the midst of troubling times. Go back to Psalm 107, this time reading verses 10-22. What happens when the rebellious heart cries out to God?

Turning our hearts back to God allows Him to break down gates of bronze and cut through bars of iron (Psalm 107:16). If you find your heart is heavy with sorrow, sin, and worry, seek God, praise God, and ask Him to penetrate your heart. He will lighten your heart. He promises!

Spiritual exercise

The way of the kingdom is poverty of spirit, gentleness, humility, and compassion. Our spirit is strengthened and renewed in our brokenness. While most of us recognize in the physical world that the reward for exercise (which can sometimes be painful) is physical strength, in God's economy His strength is built in our hearts when we acknowledge our absolute weakness without Christ.

For most of my Christian life I had this backward. I thought the best exercise for strengthening my heart was to build up a giant wall of mental toughness. Brick by brick, I was responsible for protecting my heart, and making it strong. It took a lot of muscle to make sure my wall didn't topple. The best way to stay strong? Try never to dwell on *anything* that might upset me. And certainly don't show others my weaknesses! I vowed not to cry in movies. I definitely wouldn't cry during church! Easter and Christmas services were spent biting the insides of my cheeks and thinking about anything other than what was being preached. Therefore I went through my life self-sufficient, but numb. My mantra in life was "God won't give me anything I can't handle." Read that sentence again. You can start to get pretty judgmental and self-righteous when you think you are the one keeping it all together because it's based on what *you* can handle.

God finally hit me over the head with the fallacy of that statement when I was in the midst of a crisis I couldn't handle. No amount of my own strength was going to get me through, no matter how many times I uttered my all too familiar mantra. Suddenly my wall came toppling down. That wall I had built up and held on to for dear life, kept out the only One who had the strength I sought. It is in our brokenness that He is able to rebuild our hearts. "The LORD is close to the brokenhearted; he rescues those whose spirits are crushed" (Psalm 34:18).

It's only when you exercise a brokenness of spirit that God's strength is built within your heart. Once I recognized that on my own I was doomed to a life of heart numbing self-righteousness, that I had built up a wall that kept my Creator out, the tears just fell. The tears still fall when I think of how He saved

> *The Bible never says God won't give us more than we can handle. In fact, it gives many examples of God doing just that because He **wants** us to turn to Him for help!*

me from myself. It's a daily exercise to humble myself before God and admit that I can't fix myself, and am a great big mess without Him.

Kay Warren expresses what happens when we acknowledge this:

> You can begin to offer to others what you've received from God: forgiveness, grace, mercy, acceptance, second chances, new beginnings, 'a crown of beauty instead of ashes' (Isaiah 61:3). You no longer have to live in denial of what you've done or what tempts you now. You don't have to pretend you're better than anyone else and would never do what they've done. You're free—released to be a forgiven sinner who can forgive and accept others.[9]

Talk about good fruit springing forth from good soil!

Unhealthy spiritual habits

Paul wrote in Romans 7:22-24, "I love God's law with all my heart. But there is another power within me that is at war with my mind. This power makes me a slave to the sin that is still within me. Oh, what a miserable person I am!"

Our sinful nature will always be at war with God's Word in us. There are certain sins and temptations that we will always battle within our flesh, no matter how healthy our spiritual walk.

The words of Paul in Romans 7:15 have been uttered from my own lips: "I don't really understand myself, for I want to do what is right, but I don't do it. Instead, I do what I hate."

Is there a sinful habit that you find rears its ugly head in your heart on a regular basis? (If you would rather not write it down, that's fine; but do take some time to think about those sins and temptations that you struggle with in your heart.)

_____

_____

What are some of the ways you have attempted to fight these sins on your own?

_____

_____

_____

If you, like Paul, have determined that no matter what you do, no matter how rotten you feel each time you sin, you just can't help but sin again, read Romans 7:25. Who offers us freedom from our sins?

_____

When Jesus died on the cross, He freed us from sin. He has given us His Holy Spirit to fight our sinful nature. Continue reading Romans 8:1-14 for this great reassurance.

I am so grateful to have the Holy Spirit in me to battle those sins! I have tried fighting the battle on my own. Through my own determination I may find momentary success, but without the power of the Holy Spirit I will never find long-term victory.

Don't allow Satan to deceive you by telling you that your sin is not that bad, that you can handle it on your own. *All sin*, no matter how big or small, leads to death. Satan doesn't want you to enlist the power of the Holy Spirit because he knows he will lose.

After all we have discussed about our spiritual hearts we have one last thing to consider. Psalm 44:21 says God knows the secrets of our hearts. He can peer into the deepest, darkest, most hidden places of our hearts and minds (Psalm 7:9). Regardless of what condition we think our hearts are in or how we choose to portray our hearts to the world, we can't hide anything from Him. He knows what good and evil lurks within us, and He loves us anyway. It is His desire to continually change our heart to be more like His—but He will not change our hearts without our permission.

This week, invite God to examine your heart. Ask Him to reveal areas that are not rooted in good soil. Ask him what weeds are growing in your heart, seek His forgiveness; and then with His help, pluck them out!

I can't say it any better than David does in Psalm 19:12-14: "How can I know all the sins lurking in my heart? Cleanse me from these hidden faults. Keep your servant from deliberate sins! Don't let them control me. Then I will be free of guilt and innocent of great sin. May the words of my mouth and the meditation of my heart be pleasing to you, O Lord, my rock and my redeemer."

I look forward to meeting you on the pages of our homework next week as we take a look at hitting the wall.

Week 7

Hitting the Wall

After completing this week's training and homework, you will:

- know your race pace,
- have a race day plan,
- understand God's definition of perseverance, and
- see Jesus as the perfect pacer.

Don't you realize that in a race everyone runs, but only one person gets the prize? So run to win! So I run with purpose in every step.
1 Corinthians 9:24, 26

I am so excited about our training this week! 10 miles!!! Double digits! Don't be daunted by your long run this week. You *can* do it. If you have completed most of the training so far, you are ready. It may not be easy...you might have a challenge or two...but you *can* accomplish it.

If you included a harder run during your training last week, how did it go? It's OK to feel tired after a tougher workout. It's even OK to feel sore the next day, but if you were still feeling exhausted or sore two days after your hard workout, you may want to back it off a little. There is definitely a time and place to work hard and push your limits—but if this is your first half marathon and you are struggling simply with the mileage, now is not the time to try and add speed.

Study Day One

After our "heart" felt discussion last week, let's take this week to discuss something all of us, as Christians and runners, will face at some point in our lives: Hitting the wall. For those of you who have never heard that phrase before, in runners' terms, hitting the wall means reaching the point of perceived exhaustion.

Getting through those times in your race when all you want to do it quit is one of my favorite topics. When I was training for my ultra marathon, it was the time when I desperately wanted to quit when God opened my eyes to the parallels between running and His Kingdom.

Physically, hitting the wall is simply running out of fuel. At slower paces, most of your energy comes from stored fat being turned into energy; but converting fat to fuel requires a lot of oxygen—something your muscles lack when running at higher speeds. At increased exercise intensity (race pace), your body's most efficient use of energy comes from glycogen, which comes from carbohydrates. Your body can only store a limited amount of glycogen. As you deplete your glycogen stores, your body is forced to once again convert fat to energy, which causes you to slow down. Add to this the intensely painful burning sensation in your muscles caused by accumulation of lactic acid (a by-product of the glycogen being metabolized) and you have accomplished "hitting the wall."[1]

As we touched on in Week 4, your body typically has stored enough energy to run just over an hour. One of your jobs during your 10-mile runs is to determine when you need to replenish your carbs with a gel or sports drink. Is it every four miles? Every five miles? If you wait too long to replenish your carbs, you will find that you can't maintain your race pace.

Week 7 TRAINING SCHEDULE

There are 5 workouts (4 runs, 1 cross training) and 2 rest days each week.
The workout days are flexible, however use 1 rest day after your longest run.

WEEK 7	WORKOUT 1	WORKOUT 2	WORKOUT 3	WORKOUT 4	WORKOUT 5	WORKOUT 6	WORKOUT 7
PLAN	**Easy Run** 50-60 min OR Easy Pace 10 Race Pace 20 Easy Pace 20	**X-train** 30 min + 20 min core	**Easy Run** 40 min (spend 15 min on form)	(before running, do 5 min of form exercises) **Easy Run** 45-55 min + 10 min core	**Rest**	**Long Run** 10 miles (in mile 8, do 7 strides, 30 sec each)	**Rest**
LOG							

Always spend 5-10 minutes warming up and 5-10 minutes cooling down. This can be included in your total time/mileage.

Long Run: These should be at an easy, conversational pace.

Easy Run: Easy runs should be at an easy, conversational pace. On a scale of 1-10 (10 being all out effort), an easy run should feel like a 5-6.

Race Pace: The pace you plan to run during your race as predicted on page 135.

X-train: Cross-training. Anything other than running, such as swimming, biking, walking, strength training.

LOG: This is where you write what you ACTUALLY did that day, along with a description of how you prepared and how you felt.

Core: Choose a few core exercises and spend time strengthening your core after your run.

Form: Concentrate on your running form during your run. Arms, neck, foot placement, breathing...

Form Exercises: Butt kicks and high knees.

Strides: 30-second easy sprints, keeping good form, concentrating on quick foot turnover. Allow heart rate to lower in between each stride.

Let us run with endurance the race that God has set before us. — HEBREWS 12:1

(This page is left blank so that you can cut out the workout plan on the other side and display it where you'll see it regularly.)

According to Nancy Clark, M.S., R.D., and author of *Nancy Clark's Food Guide for Marathoners*, the ideal is to take in 100 to 250 calories (or 25 to 60 grams of carbs) per hour, after the first hour of running, making sure you take it *before* you need it. That's 1 to 2 sports gels or 16 to 40 ounces of sports drink per hour.[2] So, use the next few weeks to help you determine how many gels you need and when you need them. Depending on how hard I am running, I will take 2 to 3 gels during my half-marathons, with the first one between five and six miles.

You can hit the wall mentally, as well as physically. One theory is that your brain, attempting to protect your muscles from further damage, tells your body to slow down.[3] Other research points to chemical changes in our brain that cause central nervous system fatigue and force us to slow down, even before our muscles have completely run out of fuel.[4]

If you have ever participated in a race before, have you ever hit the wall? Yes/No

If you answered yes, how did you feel? What happened to you, both physically and mentally?

_____

_____

_____

Honestly, I don't think there has ever been an event in which I truly *raced* that I didn't have some point when I wanted to quit. If I was at the start line with the intention of running my best, I could pretty much guarantee that at some point I would have the overwhelming urge to quit.

A good race plan goes a long way to helping you avoid "hitting the wall." A race plan is a well thought-out course of action that you plan to follow during your race. A race plan includes:

- pacing
- race goals
- mental strategies for getting through your rough patches

Pacing

David Costill, a noted exercise physiologist and running researcher, suggests that "hitting the wall is simply a matter of poor pacing."[5] So, how do you determine a proper race pace?

If this is your first race and you have never before run 13.1 miles, you are not going to worry about your race pace. Your first half marathon should be fun and your race pace goal should be simply to cross the finish line. Your pace will not increase much from your easy, long run pace. In other words, if your easy, long run pace for ten miles is two hours, you are running a 12-minute per mile pace. You can assume you will run about this same pace for your race. Make sure to note how long your 10-mile run takes you this week. To determine your pace per mile, you can use a pace calculator. A great pace calculator can be found at RunningByTheBook.com. Click on "Tools" and select "Pace." Use ten miles as your distance, and plug in your total running time to determine your pace per mile.

My first half marathon pace prediction:

Total time for 10-mile run _____
Pace per mile _____

If this is not your first race, the easiest way to determine an appropriate race pace is to plug a recent race time into a race calculator. A race calculator takes your finishing time from different races and determines your probable pace for another race distance. For instance, if you ran a recent 5K, you can plug in your finish time for that race and the calculator will determine what your expected half marathon race pace should be. Go to runnersworld.com and click on "Tools" then click on "Training Calculator." Plug in your previous race results, and the calculator will predict your finish time for a half marathon. I have found these prediction calculators to be pretty accurate.

Note: Race calculators only work if you have results from a *recent* race. A race result from ten years ago is not an accurate representation of what you are able to run today.

My first half marathon pace prediction:

Recent previous race distance _____

Finish time _____

Projected half marathon race pace _____

On your training schedule this week, you will see a time in the first workout where you'll practice RP (race pace). After a good warm up, spend 10-20 minutes at your race pace. Rather than just running a bit harder like we did last week, we're now going to specifically train at race pace. This will give our bodies a chance to see what this pace feels like. As we get closer to our race, our RP runs will lengthen.

Again, if this is your first race, do not worry too much about your race pace. Your job is simply to finish!

One of the biggest mistakes runners (beginners and veterans alike) make in their race is starting out too fast. For every second you gain in the first half of your race by going faster than your goal pace, two seconds are lost in the second half.[6]

Not starting out too fast is easier said than done! It's so easy to get caught up in the excitement of the crowd. It doesn't feel like you're running too fast when the people (who, by the way, are probably starting too fast as well) around you are running the same speed. After your taper week (a week of rest before the race), your race pace may actually feel easier than it did during training; but if you start out faster than your goal pace, you will deplete your body of fuel and your overall pace will suffer.

You need to know your target race pace before you hit the starting line and stick to it—regardless of how great you feel once you start running. Let people pass you! If you stick to your race pace, more than likely you will be passing them when they run out of steam because they started too fast.

So, what are we going to stick to when we start our race, even if we feel like we can go faster?

Race goals

"Why is it that runners are disappointed with race finish times? Often it is not because of a poor performance but the result of an unrealistic goal."[7]

Setting goals based on an unrealistic finish time will result in a disappointing race. Many times people set a time goal based on something arbitrary, such as how the finish time sounds. Being able to say, "I ran a half marathon in under two hours" sounds pretty good, but if your training runs are 12-minute miles, it's unrealistic to think you can run a 9-minute mile during your race. It doesn't mean you will never be able to run a half marathon in under two hours; it just means that given your current training, this is not a realistic expectation. Even a pace just a few seconds faster than your current fitness level can result in a disappointing race.

For those of you who have raced before, it is important to recognize that you are not going to run your best race every race. Somehow that competitive part of us is convinced that each race must be faster than the last. This is simply not possible. "Those performances that produce PRs [personal records] need to be appreciated and enjoyed with an understanding that a confluence of factors contributed to that achievement."[8] It's not fair to expect every performance to equal or exceed that PR. I want you to *love* running and racing, and make it a permanent part of your lifestyle … so my job is to help you determine realistic, appropriate goals for each and every race.

Now that we have determined your race pace (or at least are in the process of getting there), we can determine a finish time goal. In fact, we're going to come up with three different, appropriate finish time goals.

Finish time #1

Go to RunningByTheBook.com, click on "Tools" and then on "Time." Select the half-marathon length and enter the goal race pace that you wrote down in the "Pacing" section above. Based on those figures, the calculator will determine your finish time. Based on recent past race performance and current long run paces, this is an achievable time goal.

Finish time goal _____

Finish time #2

This is a finish time goal that is still acceptable, but takes into account a not-so-perfect race. It should be about five minutes slower than your first goal.

Finish time goal _____

Finish time #3

Your last finish time goal is when everything goes better than expected, and is slightly faster than what you think you can accomplish. It should be about five minutes faster than your finish time #1.

Finish time goal _____

Now you have three solid, appropriate finish times. While you are shooting for finish #1, if things don't go quite as planned, you are still happy with #2; and if everything is perfect on race day, you'd be thrilled with goal #3.

Performance goals

The runners in Disney's half marathon in 2010 woke up to 20-degree weather and sleet. You read that right—it *sleeted* in Orlando, Florida. The ground at the water stations was sheets of black ice, and the cups of water were frozen solid. Attempting a time goal under those conditions would have been downright dangerous.

Maybe you wake up to perfect race day weather, only to discover that you have a scratchy throat and a drippy nose that might just be the beginnings of a cold. The finish time goals you set may no longer be practical. It's races like these where you must reconsider your finish time, and instead focus on performance goals.

Performance goals take into account the type of experience you would like to have on race day, regardless of your finish time. In fact, I recommend that for first time racers, setting performance-based goals are more important than finish time goals. Besides, your first race is automatically your best time ever!

Here are some examples of good race performance goals:

- ☑ Feel good at the finish.
- ☑ Have a great time.
- ☑ Learn something new about myself.
- ☑ Give it my all.
- ☑ Persevere.
- ☑ Stay injury free.
- ☑ Motivate someone else to keep running.

☑   Finish for a specific cause.

☑   _____

☑   _____

☑   _____

In every race I run, one of my performance goals is to persevere, regardless of what race day throws my way. To cross that finish line, no matter how long it takes me.

Take a few minutes to determine two or three performance goals you have for this race. You can circle any above, or write in your own.

Race day strategies

One of the reasons the half marathon is my favorite race is because it is accessible to so many people. Most people can find the time to successfully train for—and finish—the race. A half marathon requires perseverance in training and endurance to cross the finish line, but it does not require hours and hours of running each week. All of the parts of our spiritual walk are paralleled, from training plans, to faith, to building up our temples, to emotionally hitting the wall, and persevering to the finish line.

At some point in your race, your body and mind are going to fatigue. It's an inevitable part of racing. In fact, if you don't feel like quitting at some point, you're probably not running hard enough. The key is to expect the fatigue, and endure in spite of it.

Dr. Timothy Noakes has this to say about race fatigue:

> Near the end of any race, regardless of its distance, fatigue becomes a real issue...the solution is to adopt the associating form of mental imagery and to segment the remaining race distance into manageable segments...you can then focus all your efforts of getting through

the next race segment without any concern about the total distance still remaining.[9]

In other words, you can get to the finish line by breaking the race down into smaller segments and concentrating on just getting through that next half mile or mile. Within each race segment, using a combination of associative and dissociative thought strategies appear to work best for most non-professional runners.

Associative strategies require the runner to stay in the present. To "concentrate purely on the activity and how your body feels as you run."[10] **Dissociative strategies** entail thinking about *anything* but running, instead focusing on interacting with other runners and spectators, and just enjoying the scenery.[11]

I agree with Dr. Noakes. I find that a combination of being aware of how my body feels, and taking my mind off of what I am doing by enjoying my surroundings and thinking about the reasons why I am running, enables me to not only race well, but enjoy the process. As my mind and body tire, I concentrate on the next half mile. I check my form and breathing; then I take a look around and enjoy the race. I smile and wave to the spectators who are cheering me on. I thank the race volunteers. I think about how blessed I am to be able to run. I praise God for Jesus in my life.

Counselors often suggest dissociative strategies when we're going through difficulties. Instead of focusing on our own problems, we often improve our situation and outlook by focusing on how we can help others with their difficulties!

I think about the pain I feel and how it is nothing compared to the suffering Jesus endured on the cross. At the next mile marker, I start that process over.

So, what is it going to take for you to finish your race? When you get to miles 10, 11, and 12, what are you going to feed your mind in order to keep your feet moving forward? Only you can determine what it will take to get you across that finish line. You can't wait until you are struggling at mile 11 to figure it out, so take the time to do so now:

My race strategy:

_____

_____

_____

What I will think about as I concentrate on my running (associative strategy)?

_____

_____

What I will think about as I enjoy the race around me (dissociative strategy)?

_____

_____

Being prepared for the struggle in your race will help you get to the finish line. We will build on this, and how positive thoughts affect our race when we discuss cognitive restructuring in Week 9.

Study Day Two

And let us run with endurance the race God has set before us
Hebrews 12:1

The first part of this week, we talked all about our race strategy. What are the three components of your race plan?

- _____

- _____

- _____

Hopefully you have spent some time really thinking about what it will take to get across that finish line. Before we dive into today's lesson on perseverance, let's take a few minutes to look at the spiritual implications of our race plan.

Race pace

In Day One, we discussed how running too fast in the beginning of our race was a recipe for disaster in the second half of our race. I think running too fast in our spiritual journey can have the same disastrous results. Sometimes we can get so excited about God's plans for us that we run as fast as we can, thinking if we don't capitalize on it and give it everything we have as fast as possible, then it won't come to fruition. So we run full speed into our projects only to find ourselves burned out before we have reached the finish line. We forget that we are in it for the long haul. We forget to be patient.

God certainly wants us to step out in faith and move forward with Him. Our pace should be a little challenging, especially as we mature in our faith, but our pace can't be so fast that we're unable to maintain it. He doesn't want us to run so hard and fast that we lose sight of Him.

A pastor friend once warned me to never run ahead of God. He said sometimes people get so fired up about something that they think they have to get it all done as fast as possible. So they run hard and fast, only to wake up one day and discover they left God behind. God knows our lives are a marathon. He doesn't expect us to run faster than we are capable of and risk burning out.

I have to constantly remind myself that if God has truly put something on my heart, then He will make sure it is accomplished in His perfect timing—which is rarely my timing. I need to move forward diligently and patiently, at a pace I can sustain for the long haul, keeping Him in my sight. When the obstacles come, He will be there to strengthen me and help me push through to the other side. If I run too fast and lose sight of God, when I reach that wall, I won't have the energy I need to persevere and finish my race.

Race goals

I had a friend tell me she had made it her goal to read the Bible for an hour every day. While that is certainly an admirable and worthwhile goal, I knew that with two toddlers and a husband who worked 80 hours a week, this goal was probably not attainable in her current season of life. She might be able to maintain her hour-long Bible study for a day, maybe even a week, but pretty soon she would find she just couldn't spend an hour in the Word every day, given her current life circumstances. She would mentally beat herself up and probably quit opening the Bible altogether. After all, if she couldn't reach her goal, what was the point? She set herself up for failure.

Have you ever set a lofty spiritual goal, only to find you couldn't possibly attain it?

_____

_____

Why do we do that to ourselves? We set unattainable goals and then consider ourselves failures when we don't reach them. Don't misunderstand what I'm saying—setting goals that are going to stretch us in order to reach them is a good thing, but setting a goal so high we can never hope to achieve it given our current circumstances just leads to giving up and guilt. If my friend had set a goal of being in the Word every day without specifying that it had to be for an hour—hey, with two toddlers even that goal was going to stretch her!—she could have found success, which would have encouraged her to set even higher goals for herself.

Sometimes we set arbitrary goals, and in an attempt to achieve them, forget the very reason we set the goal. John Ortberg has a great example of this in his book, *The Life You've Always Wanted*. He decided to read a devotional book, and finish it by the end of the year. He said, "Several times as I read, it was clear that something was happening in my heart; I felt I should stop and study a certain passage for a while. But such delays would have kept me from my goal of finishing the book. So I kept going."[12] He allowed his arbitrary goal to prevent him from the very thing he wanted to achieve from reading the devotional book—spiritual transformation.

I have been guilty of this myself. I once set a goal of finishing *all* of my Bible study homework before class each week, but in rushing through my weekly homework to make sure every question had an answer, I missed the entire point of the study! I could hardly remember what the homework was about, and I certainly didn't allow it to sink into my heart and help me grow spiritually. We can't allow achieving our goals to undermine the reason we set them in the first place.

Race day strategies

We touched on associative and dissociative strategies, and how using a combination of these thoughts can help us through our final race miles. I have so much more to say about mentally preparing for our race that we are going to devote all of Week 9 to that subject. Until then, let's take the rest of today to dig into one of my favorite "hitting the wall" subjects: perseverance.

I love the subject of perseverance, maybe because my life is such a testimony. I have hit the wall so many times in my spiritual walk, and every time Jesus has been there to get me through; and here I am... still running!

When you think of perseverance and endurance, what comes to mind?

_____

_____

Maybe it's because I have a tendency to relate everything to running, but for the longest time when I thought of perseverance, I envisioned someone running hard, teeth gritted, muscles burning, lungs aching—the way I feel in the last few miles of a race when all I want to do is quit, but I know I have to make it to the finish line.

But this is only one dimension of perseverance. Let's take a look at one of my favorite verses to get the entire picture of perseverance.

Look up Hebrews 12:1 and fill in the blanks:
Therefore, since we are surrounded by such a great cloud of _____,
let us throw off everything that _____ *and the sin that so easily*
_____. *And let us* _____ *with* _____ *the*
_____ *for us (NIV).*

A study of the Greek words in the original Bible leads to a deeper understanding of what the writer is saying: Be encouraged by those whose lives have exemplified faith—not to be burdened by sins that prevent us from running our race, but to patiently and steadfastly spend our strength enduring the struggles that God has destined for us.
I *love* that picture of perseverance! Perseverance is steadfastly, patiently, bravely, calmly holding fast to our faith in Christ. Persevering is finding our perfect race pace for our current situation; a pace where we are working hard, running consistently and steadily, but still have enough fuel to get to the finish line. It's running in that peaceful, flowing form from Week 5, despite our suffering.

Perseverance means not expecting things to be easy. It's recognizing that struggles will come—that we might hit the wall and have moments of gritting teeth and labored breath—but knowing those moments will pass if we lean on His strength and just keep moving. It's allowing the Holy Spirit to work in us so that our sins don't weigh us down or cause us to flee, preventing us from running the race God has marked out for us. That is the perseverance—the endurance—that will get us to our finish line.

Paul used the analogy of running a race to describe the kind of perseverance our Christian walk requires. I'd like to think if he were alive today he'd enjoy running half marathons and marathons for many of the same reasons that I do.

Read the following verses. How does Paul compare running a race to our Christian walk?

1 Corinthians 9:24-27 _____

_____

Philippians 3:13-14 _____

_____

2 Timothy 2:5 _____

_____

2 Timothy 4:7-8 _____

_____

Paul endured more struggles than I ever care to experience in my lifetime, yet he "fought a good fight" and finished his race. He knew that his prize, the crown of glory, awaited him. His message to us is one of encouragement; to run our race strong, knowing that our prize is also waiting for us in Heaven. God's Word promises that we will struggle and at times we may "hit the wall."

Our struggles may be internal:
- faith and trust
- finding peace

- dealing with our weaknesses
- guarding our heart
- battling our own inappropriate desires

Our struggles may be external:
- persecution for our faith
- things beyond our control, caused by living in a fallen world
- an illness or disease
- decisions made by other people that deeply effect our lives

Look up the following Scriptures. What do they say about our struggles and suffering?

Romans 8:17-18 _____

_____

2 Corinthians 1:3-5 _____

_____

Philippians 1:29-30 _____

_____

James 1:12 _____

_____

Christ doesn't want us to merely survive our suffering. He wants us to see it as a privilege, and a blessing. He calls us to not only endure, but—through Him—to overcome so that we can be blessed. Read this incredible definition of *overcome*: "to gain the victory; win; conquer." Also "prevail over," "surmount," and "to get the better of."[13]

The goal of a proper race plan is to help you not only endure the race, but to finish feeling strong. I don't want you to merely survive your race. I want you to conquer it!

God wants us to not just survive our struggles, but to gain the victory, win, conquer, and prevail over them, finishing our race strong. We do that by following His perfect race plan for us—by allowing Jesus to be our "pacer."

Some of the bigger half marathon races have free pace groups, led by experienced pacers. A pacer's job is to get you to the finish line at a specific time. If your goal is to run a 2-hour half marathon, you can sign up for the 2-hour pace group, and a good pacer will get you across the finish line at exactly two hours.

Pacers typically run while holding a balloon or a sign announcing their expected finish time. As long as you are within a few feet of those balloons, you can be sure you will accomplish your finish goal—assuming you have properly trained for that pace and can stay with them. A pacer can't run the race for you or make up for poor training. Using a pacer is not a shortcut to the finish; it is simply a way to ease the burden of maintaining the proper race pace.

My first experience with a pace group was at a Disney marathon. There were probably 40-50 runners crowded around the pacer at the start of the race, all hoping he would help them meet their race goals. Some of the runners were afraid to totally commit to the pace group, and they hung out at the fringes. I was one of the handful of runners who introduced themselves to the pacer and determined to stay within earshot of him, to soak in the words of wisdom and encouragement he promised along the way.

The first few miles of the race were extremely crowded, and I had a difficult time staying with the group. At one point, I took my eyes off the balloons he was holding up and I lost the group completely. It took me a mile to finally catch back up. After that, I vowed I would not let him get more than three feet in front of me. As he ran in and out of the crowds, I followed right behind, keeping a watchful eye on him at all times.

I relaxed into the race, knowing the pacer's job was to keep my pace consistent and steady, mile after mile. Every mile marker we passed proved to be right on race pace.

As we ran, people saw the balloon and joined our group. They were tired of trying to keep pace on their own, and welcomed the chance to let someone more experienced take over for a while.

With each passing mile came a story of encouragement or a tidbit of racing wisdom. He gently reminded us to keep proper form, and when to take in nourishment.

Each mile saw more and more people drop from the group—people who hadn't trained well enough to run at that pace. Some announced they could no longer keep up and said goodbye. Others silently slowed their pace and disappeared into the crowd of runners behind us.

Have you connected with someone more experienced than you in the Christian race, and invited him or her to keep an eye on your life and counsel you on the pace of your own journey?

During the last few miles, when my muscles ached and my head grew fuzzy, he encouraged me to remember why I was running. When my legs felt like lead and I was sure I could no longer keep up the pace, I imagined a rope tied from his waist to mine—he pulled me toward the finish. Never once did he look tired. I could see that my pace was nothing compared to what he was capable of, and yet he was there to help me finish my race.

Just before we reached the end of the race, he dropped behind me and I crossed the finish line two steps in front of him. We finished one minute ahead of our goal.

I burst into tears, overwhelmed with the emotions of the race. Only two of us from the original pace group had made the decision to stay with him the entire way. Through my tears, I thanked my pacer. I told him how grateful I was, and that I would not have been able to finish under my goal time without him.

As I reflected on that experience later that day, I couldn't help but think that Jesus is our ultimate pacer in the only race that really matters. He knows the way and will always be there, a couple of steps ahead. It's possible to lose sight of Him, if we allow ourselves to take our eyes off of Him; but we can always find Him again because He is consistent and steadfast. If we run too far ahead of Him, we will run out of energy before we reach the finish; that pace is too fast. Staying near Him, we find our perfect pace, the pace where we will persevere and overcome to reach the finish line.

We can rely on Him for perfect timing. We can tell Him when we are in trouble, when the race is getting tough, and He will be there offering words of encouragement and wisdom. He will gently remind us of the importance of taking in nourishment because He knows we will not finish the race without the proper fuel. We need to fill up on His presence and His Word before fatigue sets in!

With open arms, He welcomes everyone to join Him, no matter how far along they are in their race; yet we have the option to drop out at any time. He won't force us to stay. And, unfortunately, many of us will drop out because we have failed to see the importance of training. Some will quit with a loud proclamation: "This race is too hard. I'm tired of keeping up!" Others will simply give in to their struggles and silently fade away.

He never grows weary, and—ever the servant—He cares more about each of us finishing our races than about Himself. Jesus suffered more in His race on earth than we can ever imagine, and conquered death to save us. He wants nothing more than to help us overcome our own race and join Him in His victory celebration. He is the ultimate pacer!

I am so excited for you to run your first ten miles this week. Practice fueling your body with gels, and feeding your mind with thoughts that will get you to your finish! Don't forget to figure out your race pace this week. I look forward to seeing you on the pages of your study next week as we discuss much-needed rest and recovery.

Week 8

Rest and Recovery

After completing this week's training and homework, you will:

- understand the importance of rest and recovery, both physically and spiritually,
- recognize the symptoms of overtraining,
- know how much extra sleep you need while training, and
- understand our need for joyous activities.

> *On the seventh day God had finished his work of creation,*
> *so he rested from all his work.*
> Genesis 2:2

So, how was your run last week? I hope you wrote in your training log how you felt, what went right, and any problems you encountered. Have you begun developing your race plan? If you can, from memory, explain the difference between associative and dissociative thought strategies that can keep you running strong as you start to fatigue:

_____

_____

_____

I know that the last couple of weeks have had some pretty challenging homework. This week will hopefully be a breath of fresh air as we talk about something we all enjoy (and most of us can probably use more of): rest and recovery. We touched on recovery during Week 4. Do you remember why we need to take a recovery week in our training? (To jog your memory, turn back to page 57.)

_____

_____

Recovery does not mean "sit on the couch and do nothing." We're still going to run this week. Recovery simply means to slow down, enjoy a nice easy pace, and run a little less mileage.

A good training plan allows for recovery within the program. Our program has three weeks of mileage building followed by a recovery week of easier, lower mileage. Our runs this week will be shorter and easier to allow our bodies to recover from our last three weeks of training. This chapter will be shorter, with only one day of homework so that you can mentally recover as well!

A rest day is just that—a day where we do not run or workout at all. The two rest days in our training plan each week are needed to give your body a chance to recover from harder workouts. These days are just as important as running days! They allow your body to restock its glycogen stores, grow stronger, and fight fatigue.[1]

Sleep is also an extremely important part of training. As our mileage increases and our runs grow progressively harder, our muscles develop microtears. It is during sleep that these microtears have a chance to heal. I can't tell you how much sleep you should get because everyone's needs are different. Dean Karnazes, the man who ran 50 marathons in 50 days, did fine on about four hours of sleep each night.[2] Olympic marathoner Paula Radcliffe sleeps nine hours a night and takes a two-hour nap each afternoon while in training.[3]

Week 8 TRAINING SCHEDULE

There are 5 workouts (4 runs, 1 cross training) and 2 rest days each week.
The workout days are flexible, however use 1 rest day after your longest run.

WEEK 8	WORKOUT 1	WORKOUT 2	WORKOUT 3	WORKOUT 4	WORKOUT 5	WORKOUT 6	WORKOUT 7
PLAN	Easy Run 40 min	X-train 30 min + 20 min core	Easy Run 35 min (spend 10 min on form)	Easy Run 45 min + 10 min core	Rest	Long Run 7 miles	Rest
LOG							

Always spend 5-10 minutes warming up and 5-10 minutes cooling down. This can be included in your total time/mileage.

Long Run: These should be at an easy, conversational pace.
Easy Run: Easy runs should be at an easy, conversational pace. On a scale of 1-10 (10 being all out effort), an easy run should feel like a 5-6.
X-train: Cross-training. Anything other than running, such as swimming, biking, walking, strength training.
LOG: This is where you write what you ACTUALLY did that day, along with a description of how you prepared and how you felt.
Core: Choose a few core exercises and spend time strengthening your core after your run.
Form: Concentrate on your running form during your run. Arms, neck, foot placement, breathing....

On the seventh day, having finished His task, God rested from all His work. — GENESIS 2:2

(This page is left blank so that you can cut out the workout plan on the other side and display it where you'll see it regularly.)

Most of us probably fall somewhere in the middle of those two extremes. The rule of thumb while training is to get one extra minute of sleep per night for every mile you run during the week. For example, if you are running a total of 20 miles per week then you need an extra 20 minutes of sleep each night.

Because of the busy lifestyles we've created, most of us have a tendency to not get enough sleep. Sleep deprivation can be devastating to your running performance. Karnazes says, "The effects of sleep deprivation are cumulative, so that even a modest amount of sleep deprivation each night can add up to big problems over time. As few as thirty hours of cumulative sleep deprivation have been shown to reduce the cardiovascular performance of runners by more than 10 percent. If you need eight hours of sleep a night and get only seven, your running may be compromised within a month."[4]

Inadequate sleep has also been linked to weight gain. When we are sleep deprived, we produce more of the hormone, ghrelin, which tells us, "I'm hungry"; and we produce less of the hormone, leptin, which tells us, "I'm full."[5] When these hormones are out of balance, we have a tendency to eat more frequently and not stop when we are full.

One way to gauge whether or not you're getting adequate sleep is how you feel during the day. If you are dragging and feel like you need a nap or a caffeine pick-me-up every afternoon, you probably need to get more sleep at night.

When you don't have enough rest, recovery, and sleep in your training, you make yourself susceptible to overtraining syndrome. **Overtraining syndrome** occurs when you have pushed your body past the point of being able to adequately recover. Instead of building your body up and getting stronger, you begin tearing your body down. As runners, we have a tendency to believe that the harder we train, the faster we will run; but if we continue to add harder miles each week without taking time to rest, we will ultimately stretch our bodies beyond their breaking points.

Here are some red flags that indicate you may be overtraining:

- extreme fatigue
- weight loss
- increased resting heart rate
- increased delta heart rate
- persistent muscle soreness
- stomach issues (especially diarrhea)
- increased susceptibility to illness
- a normally easy training run feels hard
- irritability
- loss of enthusiasm for training
- loss of appetite
- increased thirst at night
- insomnia

I am a fairly conservative coach. I prefer to train myself and my clients with a slow buildup of miles, and enough recovery in order to avoid overtraining. However, other factors can contribute to overtraining issues, including work pressures, poor nutrition, emotional stress, and lack of sleep.

I found myself on the verge of overtraining last year during the last few weeks of my marathon training. A few sleepless nights because of sick kids, poor nutrition (I was so busy with my sick kids, I was not taking the time to eat well), plus significant life stresses, and I found I was exhausted and cranky. My legs ached all the time, and just did not seem to recover from my training. I didn't even look forward to my runs.

I knew I was on my way to overtraining, so I took a couple of days off. I didn't run at all. Then after a couple of days of complete rest, I went for a run—but I ran just for fun. I didn't worry about how far, how long, or if I was following my training program. After about a week, I finally started to feel like my old self and I picked my training program back up. Had I failed to see the early signs of overtraining and not taken a break, I would have risked injury or illness—which would have set me back much more than a week of training.

If you start to see the beginning signs of overtraining, your body is telling you to slow down! Give yourself some time to rest. Ignore the signs of overtraining and your body will eventually rebel, forcing you to take off much more time than just a few days of rest and easy runs.

You don't have to search hard in the Bible to see God's thoughts on rest and recovery. Look up Genesis 2:2-3. What did God do when He finished His creation?

_____

_____

God didn't rest because He was tired. Isaiah 40:28 tells us that He doesn't grow tired or weary. He rested because He was satisfied with His creation. He rested to model for us the importance of rest in our own lives. The word Sabbath comes from the Hebrew root word *shabath*, which means to cease, desist, rest.[6]

Maybe I am revealing my ignorance, but I was surprised at this definition. All of my life, I thought Sabbath meant go to church and worship God. There is an aspect of that within this definition—church is a great place to rest and renew our souls, to be grateful for our blessings, and to worship the One who has blessed us—but Sabbath is more than just going to church.

When God spoke to Moses on Mount Sinai, His final words on that fortieth day were a reminder to the Israelites to keep the Sabbath day forever.

"It is a permanent sign of my covenant with the people of Israel. For in six days the LORD made heaven and earth, but on the seventh day he stopped working and was refreshed" (Exodus 31:17).

What a wonderful word, *refreshed*. Dictionary.com suggests such synonyms as revive, restore, renew, and repair.[7] God knows we need a day to revive, renew, repair, and restore our souls.

How many of us fill the Sabbath day with all of the activities we weren't able to get done throughout the week? I'm certainly guilty of this. On my way home from church, I stop off at the grocery store to do my weekly shopping; then I go home and prepare dinners for the following week, while cleaning the mountain of laundry that has piled up. I'm not saying we should do nothing on our Sabbath day, but perhaps we need to remind ourselves that God calls us to rest and restore once a week for a reason.

If your life is at all like mine, then it's complicated. We are pulled in so many directions, and there is always another thing to do. For most of us, the measure of a successful day is how many things we were able to check off of our to-do list. If our bodies need a chance to grow and strengthen after a hard week of running, what makes us think our souls can go and go and go without a break?

I hope by now you have begun to see that God is a God of order, of consistency. He shows us through the physical what we require spiritually. If our physical bodies require rest and recovery or they break down, then our souls do, too. Let's take a look at how we can spiritually recover, rest, and sleep.

Spiritual recovery

If a recovery run is an easy, slow paced run, then what do you think spiritual recovery should look like?

_____

_____

——————————————————————————————

——————————————————————————————

I think of spiritual recovery as slowing down our hurried pace. Putting aside our "have-to-do list" and engaging in a "want-to-do" activity—an activity that renews the joy in our hearts. Replacing a hurried, task-driven attitude with celebration of joy—an attitude like the one the psalmist has in Psalm 118:24: "This is the day the LORD has made. We will rejoice and be glad in it."

What are some activities that bring joy to your heart?

——————————————————————————————

——————————————————————————————

——————————————————————————————

——————————————————————————————

Let me tell you a few of mine: taking a hike in the mountains with my family; listening to praise music—not doing something else at the same time, but sitting still and listening; trying a new, healthy recipe for dinner; taking a walk with my dog; walking to the local coffee shop with my husband; sitting around the table eating a relaxed meal with my family; taking my Bible to a mountain overlook, and reading the Word of God surrounded by His magnificent creation; a girl's night out; reading for fun; completing a word puzzle on my Kindle; an easy trail run on a cool, sunny day. I could go on and on.

These simple activities bring me joy. They restore my soul. When I take the time to slow down and engage in a joyous activity, putting aside all of the things I "should" do, I always feel refreshed afterwards. If I do not purposefully engage in those things that fill me with joy, life easily gets in the way and I find myself feeing drained and worn out. My soul *needs* these pursuits of joy.

John Ortberg says that joy is a command of the Bible and joylessness is a sin.[8] He says we should "take the time to experience and savor joy, then direct your heart toward God so that you can come to *know* he is the giver of '*every* good and perfect gift.' Nothing is too small if it produces true joy in us and causes us to turn toward God in gratitude and delight."[9]

Spiritual rest

From the music piped in over the grocery store speakers, to the walls of televisions (each one on a different channel) at our favorite restaurants, to our own need to have the radio on in the car or the television on as background noise while we cook dinner, our lives are filled with busyness and noise. I have even known people who narrate aloud their every thought and action in order to avoid silence.

But Jesus shows us that spending time in solitude and silence refreshes our souls. Even in the midst of a busy ministry and crowds of needy people, He recognized the importance of rest. Look up the following verses and write down how Jesus found rest in each situation:

Mark 6:31-32 _____

_____

Mark 1:35 _____

_____

Luke 5:16 _____

_____

Jesus spent time alone. Throughout His ministry, we see Him retreat to solitary places to find rest in His father. Ortberg says, "At its heart, solitude is primarily about *not* doing something."[10]

It is in silence and solitude—taking time to do nothing—that our souls find rest. In a world where we have been conditioned to feel useful only when we are doing something, we may find it is actually hard to engage in the practice of *not* doing anything!

Jesus, in his periods of solitude, spent time praying and listening. Sometimes in my hustle and bustle life, I feel like all I ever do is recite a wish list of prayers I want God to answer. As I go through my busy day, I throw prayer requests at God, but forget to stop and listen.

Solitude teaches us to slow down and become fully available to God...to engage in a dialogue with our Creator, rather than a one-way speech listing our wants and needs. God is much more inclined to whisper in our hearts while we are silent and available than to shout over the empty noise of stereos and televisions or the drone of our unending prayer requests.

Spiritual sleep

Rest also includes sleep. Jesus knew the importance of getting adequate sleep. Read Matthew 8:23-25, Mark 4:35-39, and Luke 8:23.

Each disciple has his own version of this event. What do all three say Jesus was doing when the storm developed?

Even in the midst of a storm, He slept. He knew that in order to effectively minister to those around Him, He needed to take some time to close his eyes and sleep.

Contrast that to the disciples in Matthew 26:36-41. In Jesus' greatest hour of need, the disciples couldn't keep their eyes open. Jesus asked them to keep watch with Him, and they kept falling asleep on the job.

I would say that they were slightly sleep deprived. We talked about the physical effects of sleep deprivation, from weight gain to poor running performance, but sleep deprivation has spiritual consequences, as well. Think about a time you were sleep deprived. How did you feel, physically and emotionally?

_____

_____

_____

I am one irritable person when I don't have enough sleep. My emotions are magnified. The tiniest setback creates irrational discouragement, and the smallest things get on my nerves. I am certainly not very grateful or loving. I can't even engage in prayer effectively. Like the disciples in the garden at Gethsemane, I keep falling asleep.

When the prophet Elijah fled to the wilderness in 1 Kings 19:5, he had experienced a pretty hectic day. He mocked the prophets of Baal in front of the people gathered at Mt. Carmel. He built an altar to the Lord using 12 stones and wood. He dug a trench, slaughtered a bull, and cut it into pieces as a sacrifice. He prayed aloud for God to show Himself mighty. He killed 450 prophets of Baal; then he ran the 13 miles back to town, only to discover that if he stayed he would be killed. What a day!

Emotionally discouraged and physically exhausted, Elijah begged God to end his life. According to 1 Kings 19:5-7, what was the Lord's response to Elijah?

_____

_____

_____

God allowed him to nap and eat; not just once, but twice! God knows that sometimes what we need most is sleep and proper nutrition. "God gives rest to his loved ones" (Psalm 127:2). Sometimes the best thing we can do for ourselves and for God is to eat a healthy meal and go to bed earlier.

There are seasons in life when we will find ourselves emotionally and physically exhausted. Newborn babies...sick toddlers...new puppies... stress at work...a rough time in our marriage...a rebellious teen...a parent

160

with Alzheimer's. It's unrealistic to expect that we'll never endure periods when we're wrung out.

It is during these times of greatest stress that we need to fiercely protect our time spent on those activities that bring us joy, our times of solitude, and our sleep. It is in His rest and His joy that we are strengthened.

Enjoy your week of recovery. Turn off the noise around you and spend some solitary time with God. Rediscover those activities that fill your heart with joy! I can't wait to see you on the pages of your homework next week, rested and ready to tackle another week of training and running!

Cognitive Restructuring

After completing this week's training and homework, you will:

- know how and why to visualize the course regularly before your race,
- be able to focus on what's in your control and let go of everything else,
- see how changed attitudes bring about changed behaviors, and
- know how to replace negative, false thoughts with constructive, encouraging truths.

Let us throw off everything that hinders and the sin that so easily entangles. And let us run with perseverance the race marked out for us.
Hebrews 12:1 (NIV)

I hope you are rested and ready for another week of harder training. We are going to run double-digit mileage again! Make sure you prepare the day before your long run by drinking plenty of water (your urine should be *pale* yellow) and eating foods that will give your body the proper nutrients to feed your run. Look back at Week 4 for suggestions if you have forgotten what foods are best to eat and when to eat them. This week, during one of your shorter runs, count your cadence again and record it on your training log.

Last week did you take advantage of our short homework and training and engage in an activity that brings you joy? Yes / No

What activity did you participate in? How did you feel afterwards?

_____

_____

I know it may seem selfish to take time to participate in activities that fill your spirit with joy, but as Christians we are called to be "the light of the world" (Matthew 5:14). The love of Jesus that is inside us should pour out so that people are drawn to us. How can we expect to exude His joy if we do not experience joy ourselves?

Experiencing joy is an awesome reminder of how God has blessed us in the big and the small. My soul sings with praise for the Lord during a trail run or a hike. His glory is all around me! I can't help but thank God for my blessings while playing a game with my kids; and, sometimes, I experience quite a bit a joy in a small bowl of ice cream (with hot fudge sauce, if I have my way). I don't think there is anything wrong with really savoring a treat now and then; but when you do indulge, enjoy it! Don't just gulp it down as fast as possible and then feel guilty about how much you ate. Take your time, enjoy each bite; and then, thank God for the gift of your taste buds and the invention of ice cream.

Study Day One

This week we are going to look at what we learned in Week 7—the idea of our race plan and how to avoid hitting the wall—and take it to the next level as we go over the concept of mental training. Read any running book and you will find at least one chapter devoted to mental training. Even the best

Week 9 TRAINING SCHEDULE

There are 5 workouts (4 runs, 1 cross training) and 2 rest days each week.
The workout days are flexible, however use 1 rest day after your longest run.

WEEK 9	WORKOUT 1	WORKOUT 2	WORKOUT 3	WORKOUT 4	WORKOUT 5	WORKOUT 6	WORKOUT 7
PLAN	**Easy Run** 50-60 min OR Easy Pace 10 Race Pace 30 Easy Pace 10	**X-train** 30 min + 20 min core	**Easy Run** 35 min (spend 10 min on form)	*(before running, do 5 min of form exercises)* **Easy Run** 45-55 min + 10 min core	Rest	**Long Run** 10 miles (in mile 8, do 7 strides, 30 sec each)	Rest
LOG							

Always spend 5-10 minutes warming up and 5-10 minutes cooling down. This can be included in your total time/mileage.

Long Run: These should be at an easy, conversational pace.
Easy Run: Easy runs should be at an easy, conversational pace. On a scale of 1-10 (10 being all out effort), an easy run should feel like a 5-6.
Race Pace: The pace you plan to run during your race as predicted on page 135.
X-train: Cross-training. Anything other than running, such as swimming, biking, walking, strength training.
LOG: This is where you write what you ACTUALLY did that day, along with a description of how you prepared and how you felt.
Core: Choose a few core exercises and spend time strengthening your core after your run.
Form: Concentrate on your running form during your run. Arms, neck, foot placement, breathing...
Form Exercises: Butt kicks and high knees.
Strides: 30-second easy sprints, keeping good form, concentrating on quick foot turnover. Allow heart rate to lower between each set.

Do not conform to the pattern of this world, but be transformed by the renewing of your mind. Then you will be able to test and approve what God's will is — his good, pleasing and perfect will. — ROMANS 12:2 (NIV)

(This page is left blank so that you can cut out the workout plan on the other side and display it where you'll see it regularly.)

athletes need to train their minds, as well as their bodies. Our minds have tremendous power. Negative thoughts and self-doubt can undermine our physical abilities.

Kara Goucher, a 10,000 meter finalist in the 2008 Olympics, was overcome with thoughts of "I don't belong here, I'm not good enough to be here" at the starting line of her race. According to her coach, she lost that race in her mind before the starting gun even fired. Just a few months later, in her very first marathon attempt, she placed third in the 2008 New York City Marathon. She was the first American woman to stand on the winner's podium in 14 years—yet the day before that race, she told her coach she doubted she could even run the 26.2 miles.[1]

Here is an obviously talented young woman whose mind gets the best of her and prevents her from performing her best on race day. To help Kara overcome her self-defeating inner dialogue, her coach hired a sports psychologist. While we may never come close to standing on the winner's podium, we, too, can benefit from learning how to take our negative self-talk and turn it into a positive thought that propels us to our finish line. We're going to look at four mental strategies that we can utilize in our race:

1. Visualization

We talked about the importance of being familiar with your racecourse in Week 6. Do you remember why it is important to be familiar with your course ahead of time?

_____

_____

Knowing how the course is laid out also helps you utilize the technique of **visualization**. Visualization is running the race mentally—in your head—before you actually do so physically. For example, if you have a hill to climb in mile eight, picture yourself successfully running up that hill, getting to the top, and feeling strong.

According to Tim Noakes, the key is to prepare mentally for when the pain will begin—which, in the case of a half-marathon, is typically after mile 10.[2] If you have a strong mental picture of your race from mile 10 to the finish line, when the running gets tough, you will be prepared. Noakes says, "An interesting recent finding is that thinking about a specific exercise task produces the same brain activity that occurs when the actual task is being performed."[3] In other words, when you create the vivid mental image of running those last 3.1 miles, you are training your brain to successfully finish the race!

I think it's important to not only imagine running the perfect race, but to also visualize what you will do when your race isn't going so well. It's easy to create an image of the "perfect race," where your pace is strong, nothing hurts, and you feel like you're flying on air. It's much more effective to imagine what you will do when your legs ache, your chest hurts, and all you want to do is stop. If you imagine how you will feel during those last miles and visualize persevering through it, you will have a better chance of successfully navigating through your rough patches when the actual race happens. As you imagine running those last painful miles, decide now that you are not going to quit.

As you visualize the final miles of your race, what obstacles do you envision? How are you going to persevere through them?

_____

_____

_____

_____

Although I would like to think that my kids will never be exposed to alcohol or drugs, the sad truth is, at some point, they will most likely be pressured to drink or try drugs. I tell my kids they need to prepare in advance for their response. They need to visualize what they will say, and how their friends may react. How are they going to remove themselves from that situation? The time to decide what they stand for and what they will do is now, before they are actually in that situation. The decision to say no has already been made; and they are prepared to act, even before they are confronted with that choice. Make the decision to say no now when your body tries to tell you it's time to quit running.

Let's think about the spiritual aspect of this technique as well. God has given us a road map for our lives. We discovered that several weeks ago in our first week as we learned about His training plan for each of us. Within that training plan are tools we can use to navigate successfully through life's struggles— core principles we can stand on when the world around us is crumbling. If we don't know ahead of time how we are going to respond as Christians to life's challenges, it's very easy to just give up and walk away. When challenges come, do you imagine running to Christ, to His Word? Do you cling to the truths of His Word: He is good, He is unfailing, He has a plan? Are there specific verses in the Bible that offer you strength?

Decide now that you will finish your life's race. Visualize running to Christ while in the midst of your struggles. What do you visualize when you think of clinging to God when you hit a rough patch in your life? Take some time to really picture that in your mind. What do you imagine?

_____

_____

_____

_____

I have certain areas in my life that I know are going to be struggles for me—my cross to bear, you might say. Although I do my best to avoid putting myself in situations where I have to face those demons, there are times when it is unavoidable. However, I mentally rehearse how I am going to respond when faced with my struggles. I decide beforehand how I am going to resist those temptations. I back up my decision with Bible verses and prayer because it is only through relying on His strength that I will truly resist my temptations. Take time to visualize and prepare for the areas in your life that you know are a struggle. Choose to walk down your road with Jesus. Imagine what that looks like!

2. Focus on what you can control
No matter how prepared you may be, there are always going to be race factors outside of your control. We touched on this a little when we determined our race goals in Week 7. What are some things we can't control when it comes to race day?

_____

_____

On race day, your job is to focus on those things you do have control over and let go of those things that you can do nothing about. You can control what you eat for breakfast, and when you take in nutrients on the course. You can control your beginning pace. You can control your attitude. You can't control the weather, the people around you, or the people in charge of the race. Run *your* best race, based on the goals you have already set and the training you have done, and don't worry about those things out of your control.

Jesus asks us in Matthew 6:27: "Can all your worries add a single moment to your life?" Read Matthew 6:25-34 and Luke 12:22-31. What does Jesus say about worry in these Scriptures?

_____

_____

_____

_____

_____

I don't think Jesus is saying we should just sit back and wait for God to provide all of our needs, and I don't think He is saying we should never set goals or plan for tomorrow. God's desire is for us to actively discover and participate in His plan for us, to make Him a priority, and trust in His guidance. Worrying only brings immobilization and a weak finish. Trust that His plan for you is sufficient. Take control of your attitudes and choices, and let God handle the rest!

3. Allow for the unexpected

We mentioned in Week 7 that even with the best race plan in the world, even if you have done every bit of training exactly as written, things may not go according to your plan during the race. Maybe you have an unexpected detour to the bathroom, or a 20-mph head wind kicks in for three miles along the ocean; maybe a muscle that you have never had issues with suddenly starts to scream at mile eight.

If you are not able to readjust your plans and goals according to what is going on around you, your perfect race may turn into a perfectly terrible race. Running a successful race requires being willing to adjust your race goals, pace, and strategies on the fly; then take what you have learned to reset your goals for next time.

For our 10-year anniversary, my sweet husband spent close to a year planning a surprise trip to the Colorado mountains for a week of hiking, biking, and horseback riding. He arranged for his mom and sister to take care of the kids while we were gone. He researched the weather and picked the ideal week. He spent hours scouring the Internet for available cabins, local activities, and gear we would need. He planned our trip almost to the minute—all without me even knowing about it! He even went so far as to pay an extra $300 in rebooking fees when it looked as though the week we were going to go might have rotten weather after all.

When I finally found out about the trip, all I had to do was pack my bags—and he even had a list of things we should pack. It was such an amazing surprise! Unfortunately, even with all of his fastidious planning and the last minute change of dates, when we got to Colorado it was unseasonably cold, cloudy, and grey. We woke up most days to freezing rain and snow. To top it off, I spent one night throwing up in the bathroom from something I ate, which made the entire next day a little rough. Let's just say that our trip did not end up exactly the way he planned. He spent the entire week frustrated and grumpy, worrying about things he simply could not have planned for and had no control over.

4. *Treat every race as a learning experience*

Dagney Scott says, "Within every run, there are successes and defeats. You learn that you can make a conscious decision to focus on either the negative or the positive."[4] You get to choose: are you going to dwell on what went wrong during your race, or are you going to learn from what happened and use that information to reset your goals for your next race?

My dear husband has learned from that trip. He still plans our trips (he is great at that!), but he is able to readjust and go with the flow when the need arises. We have taken many trips since then, and each one has been wonderful—in spite of things not always going according to plan.

As we embrace the runner in us through our training and our races, and as we learn from our mistakes and our failures, ultimately our behaviors should change. Those habits we may have had before—an unhealthy diet, lack of sleep, and/or exercise—will no longer appeal to us because of the way they negatively affect our training. Before we became runners, we may have thought nothing about staying up into the wee hours of the morning, watching movies and gorging on popcorn, soda, and candy every Friday night.

But when our Saturday runs suffer (or we suffer during them!), we soon learn from our mistakes and see that our Friday night escapades negatively affect our early Saturday runs. Eventually, we may find ourselves substituting a glass of water for that bottle of soda, and find we choose to forgo that second movie and go to bed earlier. Maybe we start cooking healthier Friday night meals because Saturday's run is easier with better food in our systems. At first these choices may simply be out of obligation, but eventually we will find that we willingly, gladly change our behaviors because we see the fruit of our training.

As we submit our lives to God and learn from our past mistakes, our behaviors should also change. Those sins that so entangled us, as Hebrews 12:1 describes it, should no longer hold the appeal they once did. As we submit to His plan for us and our relationship with Him deepens, so will our desire to leave our sinful ways behind and follow Him.

God doesn't expect perfection, simply a heart after Him and the perseverance to learn from our mistakes. If He expected perfection, He would have never chosen the Israelites as His people in the first place! Nehemiah lists the mistakes the people of Israel repeated over and over in Nehemiah 9:7-31. Read these verses and list a few of the mistakes the Israelites made throughout history.

_____

_____

_____

_____

And yet, God is "a God of forgiveness, gracious and merciful, slow to become angry, and rich in unfailing love" (Nehemiah 9:17). Jesus knew when He chose Peter as His disciple that Peter would deny Him. Although Peter claimed in Luke 22 to be prepared to die for Jesus, what was Jesus' response in verse 34?

_____

_____

Peter failed Jesus miserably that night—as a follower and as a friend, but Peter also learned first hand about true forgiveness and enduring love through his mistake. He spent the rest of his days encouraging Christians to endure persecution for their faith and penned two books of the Bible.

Yet even as one of the first leaders of the Christian church, he still messed up. Read Galatians 2:11-16. What mistake had Peter (also called Cephas) made this time, according to Paul?

_____

_____

I pray that I am humble enough to accept my mistakes, learn from them, and use my experience to glorify God's Kingdom, don't you?

Before we finish today, take a few minutes and visualize your physical race. Go to the race Web site and study the final three miles of the course, if it is available. Vividly imagine running those final miles. Your legs feel like lead, your belly aches, and you really just want to quit. What are you going to do to keep running?

_____

_____

_____

_____

_____

_____

Study Day Two

Do not conform to the pattern of this world, but be transformed by the renewing of your mind. Then you will be able to test and approve what God's will is—his good, pleasing and perfect will.
Romans 12:2 (NIV)

Earlier this week we discussed four ways to mentally prepare for, and push through, your race. If you can, without looking, write down those four techniques:

1) _____

2) _____

3) _____

4) _____

Today we are going to go over one more strategy for training our brain for our race. This technique happens to be one of my favorites. As a matter of fact, God showed me how I could use this technique to help me breakthrough some of my toughest spiritual struggles. I hope you will find it to be just as helpful in your own spiritual life!

Cognitive restructuring

In psychological jargon, **cognitive restructuring** is the process of learning to replace faulty thinking and irrational, counter-factual beliefs with more accurate and beneficial ones.[5] That means taking the thoughts "I can't finish this race" or "I don't have the energy to make it up this hill," and learning to turn them into "I have done the training. I can finish it" and "I am going to power through this hill because I trained on hills."

Cognitive restructuring doesn't mean lying or exaggerating what you are capable of. You can't positively think yourself into a faster pace than you are trained for.[6] Cognitive restructuring is about replacing faulty, irrational thoughts with the truth.

I think it's fair to say we all have struggled with irrational, negative thoughts at some point during our training. If left unchecked, as race day gets closer, those negative thoughts can grow stronger and stronger, affecting our performance.

The negative comment I tend to hear the most is right at the beginning of training: "I could never run 13.1 miles." *That is just not true for most people.* With proper training, patience, and perseverance, most people who decide to run a half marathon are successful.

Go back to page 167 and reread the self-defeating thoughts Kara Goucher had during the Olympic finals. Using cognitive restructuring, how could she have replaced those with positive thoughts to empower her race?

_____

_____

_____

_____

I might restructure her thoughts this way: "I earned my place here by running well. I deserve to be here as much as anyone else." That may look easy enough to do on paper, but it takes practice to be able to turn a negative thought into a beneficial thought while in the heat of battle. First you have to recognize the faultiness of the thought, and then you have to determine how to turn that thought into one that motivates you and encourages you.

Sometimes an easy way to transition into this is with what runners call a mantra. A running mantra is an encouraging, uplifting word or sentence that you can focus on when your race gets tough; a word or phrase that will evoke a feeling or sensation that will pull you along.[7]

Good examples are words and phrases such as "Fight!" or "I am strong!" It has to be a short sentence—one that your brain can easily remember in the last miles of your race. It has to be something you believe. In other words, choosing "push harder" isn't going to be as successful when you don't think you have it in you to push harder. A better choice is "one foot in front of the other."[8]

I once picked Psalm 18:32-33, 36 as my mantra for a mountainous ultra marathon:

God arms me with strength,
  and he makes my way perfect.
He makes me as surefooted as a deer,
  enabling me to stand on mountain heights.
You have made a wide path for my feet
  to keep them from slipping.

Those words motivated me to my core. I memorized them, meditated on them, and felt God's protection when I recited them. Unfortunately, I realized that after a couple hours into my training runs, I could no longer remember the verse! (Your brain, depleted of oxygen, can't easily recall things after running for that long.) So I chose that verse as my ultra marathon theme verse; but chose two different, but equally powerful, words as my mantra for the rest of my training runs and race: "Stay Strong," the title of my favorite song by the Newsboys. (I'm sure it's not a coincidence that my favorite song happens to mention running in the chorus.)

I love what the Bingham High School's track and cross country coaches teach their runners about negative thoughts. The minute a negative thought enters their mind, whether before or during a race, the kids are taught to scream out loud "STOP!" They then replace that negative thought with their personal mantra.[9] The act of saying "STOP!" out loud helps the kids to stop the negative thought immediately and replace it quickly with their positive mantra.

While you may not feel comfortable yelling "STOP!" in the middle of your race for the world to hear, perhaps just thinking "STOP" will help you restructure your thoughts!

Let's take a few minutes to write down some of the negative thoughts that enter your head when you think of your race. Include the negative thoughts you may have encountered while training; then, beside them, use cognitive restructuring to rephrase those thoughts into a beneficial and motivating thought. I will do one as an example:

Negative thought	Restructured thought
I haven't done enough training. I am not ready for this race. There is no way I can run the whole race at my race pace.	I did just the right amount of training. I am not overtrained, but I am prepared. I did at least 90% of the training program, so I know I am properly prepared. I will stick to my goal pace because I know I am trained for it.

Now list yours, and the restructured thoughts you'll replace them with:

Negative thought	Restructured thought

Negative thought	Restructured thought

Now pick a key word or sentence that will motivate you when the race gets tough. Remember to keep it short and simple.

During one of my half marathon training sessions, I invited a friend and sports psychologist to speak to the group of runners I was training. As he spoke about cognitive restructuring and mantras, it hit me: the apostle Paul was talking about cognitive restructuring when he said, "Fix your thoughts on what is true, and honorable, and right, and pure, and lovely, and admirable. Think about things that are excellent and worthy of praise" (Philippians 4:8).

Yes, Paul is saying that what we allow into our minds should be honorable because, as we discussed in Week 6, what we allow into our minds flows out of our hearts. But I think it goes deeper than that. So often we allow irrational, counter-factual beliefs to hinder us from fully experiencing the deep love and abundant life God has planned for us. Dr. William Backus, a Christian psychologist, describes those thoughts as "fallacies, errors, distortions, exaggerations, and other falsehoods."[10]

Backus goes on to explain the concept biblically. "The *New Testament* word for *repent* means, literally, *change your mind.*"[11] The good news of the Gospel consists of truths that can change and renew our spirits, souls and bodies.[12] Through repentance, or the changing of our minds for the better, we can then allow the eternal truths of God's word to replace the thoughts and attitudes that wear down our spirit.[13]

> *"Search me, O God, and know my heart;*
>
> *test me and know my anxious thoughts."*
>
> *Psalm 139:23*

Remember back to our discussion on spiritual compensations in Week 5? We discussed the ways we compensate for our areas of spiritual weakness. If you need to, quickly review pages 93-94 to refresh your memory.

When we invite God to reveal those weaknesses to us and then repent (i.e. change our minds about how to deal with them), God's Word can help us replace those thoughts with His eternal truths. Let's examine a weakness that many of us struggle with on a regular basis: fear of rejection.

The first stop on my journey to replace my fear of rejection with God's truth is a thesaurus: to look up the synonyms and antonyms for *rejection.* According to a thesaurus, some antonyms of *reject* and *rejection* are "accept, allow, approve, and choose."[14] Looking a little deeper, I see that "reject" and "abandon" are synonyms. Antonyms for *abandon* include "adopt" and "favor."[15]

Remember, I am trying to replace that negative, false feeling of rejection with God's truth. I want to fill my mind with words that dispel the lies of my current thoughts. Now I can go to my Bible concordance or online resources such as biblegateway.com and search for verses that include the words *accept, allow, approve, choose, cherish, adopt,* and *favor.*

Write each of the verses I found in my Bible search:

Psalm 30:5 (favor) _____

_____

Isaiah 43:10 (chosen) _____

_____

Deuteronomy 14:2 (chosen) _____

_____

John 15:16 (choose) _____

_____

Romans 8:15-17 (adoption) _____

_____

Aren't those verses amazing? Those verses will fill your mind with His truth! If this is one of your struggles, then highlight these verses, write them in your journal, write them on index cards and post them on your fridge and mirrors—do whatever you need to do to make these verses your own, until God's truth replaces those feelings of rejection.

Let's try this again with another weakness that many of us struggle with: needing be in control. When I search the thesaurus, I find that some antonyms for *control* are "give up, let go, relinquish, resign."[16] When I think about these words, God's true desire is for me to give up my control to Him, to relinquish control of my life to Him.

If I go back to the thesaurus with the thought that God is the one in control, what other words can be used in my search? I found the synonyms "authority" and "guidance."[17] Now let's look for verses in the Bible that will fill our minds with the eternal truth that God is in control.

Matthew 28:18 (authority) _____

_____

Philippians 3:20-21 (control) _____

_____

Colossians 2:10 (authority) _____

_____

Taking the time to research words and their synonyms and antonyms is an incredible tool to help you find meaningful verses.

Now I want you to take some time to do your own research on that weakness you wrote down on page 96 of Week 5. Ask God to lead you to words and verses that will fill your heart and mind with His truth. Be creative and dig deep as you research the thesaurus, then spend time digging into your Bible for those verses that God can use to truly transform your heart.

My weakness:

_____

Synonyms: _____

_____

Antonyms: _____

_____

Verses: _____

_____

_____

_____

_____

_____

_____

_____

Once we realize that our repentance, the act of changing our mind, isn't a one-time thing, but the "daily confronting false and inadequate views of God, which result in wrong thoughts and actions on our part,"[18] we will start to become successful at filling our minds, hearts, and souls with His truths. We must actively participate in allowing God to change our hearts and minds on a daily basis.

As you run this week, don't allow negative thoughts to control your mind. Stop them and replace them with positive thoughts. Use your mantra to help you push through any tough spots on your run. I can't wait to see you on the pages of your homework next week!

Week 10

Building Up
and Tearing Down

After completing this week's training and homework, you will:

- understand the reversibility principle,
- understand progressive overload,
- recognize that discomfort is a part of growth, and
- have the base needed to run a half marathon!

> *All praise to the God, the Father of our Lord Jesus Christ,*
> *who has blessed us with every spiritual blessing in the heavenly realms*
> *because we are united with Christ.*
> Ephesians 1:3

I hope your 10-mile run went well for you! If it didn't, don't worry; you have the chance to redeem it during this week's long run because we are going to run 10 miles again. After this week's long run, you will have run 10 miles three times, which means you will be prepared to run a half marathon! That's quite an accomplishment, and you should be very proud of yourself.

Did you have the opportunity to use your mantra during your last long run? How about taking any negative thoughts and replacing them with truth? Mantras and cognitive restructuring are powerful tools when you learn how to use them effectively, and that comes with practice. If your mantras were effective during your last long run, plan to use them again. Or if they really didn't do much for you, take this opportunity to try a couple of new ones.

This week's long run is your last chance to solidify your pre-run and during-run fuel plan. The night before your long run, make sure to eat a normal-sized meal with plenty of carbs and a little lean protein. A couple of good choices are pasta with tomato sauce and lean ground beef or a small chicken breast, or rice with veggies and chicken or tofu. Don't eat anything super spicy, greasy, or unusual because your tummy may rebel in the morning! Don't forget to hydrate all day long, sipping water throughout the day.

> *Remember that a half-marathon is 30% longer than the 10 miles you're running now. Even if you haven't had tummy issues so far, you could at that distance—so make easily digestible meals a habitual part of your race plan now.*

Most half marathons occur early in the morning, so try to schedule your long run in the morning so you can practice your pre-race routine. Plan on eating at least one hour before your run. Really, 3–4 hours is better, but it can be tough to do that if you plan to run at 6 a.m.! Remember, if your stomach is empty you won't be able to sustain runs lasting more than an hour. A meal of some easily digestible carbs along with a little protein is your best bet—and the earlier you eat, the more you can eat. Think bagel with peanut butter, or banana and yogurt, or instant oatmeal and non-fat milk. Sip on water as you eat. If you are used to drinking coffee, go ahead—it may send you to the bathroom, which is always welcome before a long run.

During your long run, practice drinking the sports drink available at the race and taking gels with water. Taking in 100–250 calories of carbs per hour

Week 10 TRAINING SCHEDULE

There are 5 workouts (4 runs, 1 cross training) and 2 rest days each week.
The workout days are flexible, however use 1 rest day after your longest run.

WEEK 10	WORKOUT 1	WORKOUT 2	WORKOUT 3	WORKOUT 4	WORKOUT 5	WORKOUT 6	WORKOUT 7
PLAN	Easy Run 50-60 min OR Easy Pace 10 Race Pace 30 Easy Pace 10	X-train 30 min + 20 min core	Easy Run 35 min (spend 10 min on form)	(before running, do 3 min of form exercises) Easy Run 45-55 min + 10 min core	Rest	Long Run 10 miles (in miles 5-9 run at Race Pace)	Rest
LOG							

Always spend 5-10 minutes warming up and 5-10 minutes cooling down. This can be included in your total time/mileage.

Long Run: These should be at an easy, conversational pace.
Easy Run: Easy runs should be at an easy, conversational pace. On a scale of 1-10 (10 being all out effort), an easy run should feel like a 5-6.
Race Pace: The pace you plan to run during your race as predicted on page 135.
X-train: Cross-training. Anything other than running, such as swimming, biking, walking, strength training.
LOG: This is where you write what you ACTUALLY did that day, along with a description of how you prepared and how you felt.
Core: Choose a few core exercises and spend time strengthening your core after your run.
Form: Concentrate on your running form during your run. Arms, neck, foot placement, breathing...
Form Exercises: Butt kicks and high knees.

Praise be to the God and Father of our Lord Jesus Christ, who has blessed
us in the heavenly realms with every spiritual blessing in Christ. — EPHESIANS 1:3 (NIV)

(This page is left blank so that you can cut out the workout plan on the other side and display it where you'll see it regularly.)

while running will help you perform better; and remember to eat a small snack of carbs and protein within an hour after your run to help speed recovery. A glass of chocolate milk, a bowl of cereal, or a smoothie are all good choices.

Write down what you ate before, during, and after your run in your training log. If things didn't go so well, you can change what you ate; if things went great, you can look back and repeat your routine.

This is the last long run before your race! Hang in there with your training. If you're feeling weary and ready for your training to be over, go back to Week 7 and reread Study Day Two. Now is not the time to quit; now is the time to push through your training and persevere! You can also go back through your training logs (which I know you have been diligently filling out) and look at the progress you have made. My training log always inspires me to keep pushing once I see how far I've really come. You are so very close to victory! Stay strong!

Study Day One

This week we are going to explore two concepts that will help us recognize the value of consistent and increased training—both physically and spiritually: the reversibility principle and progressive overload. We'll start today with the bad news and pick you back up in day two with the good news.

The **reversibility principle** says that training adaptations will gradually decline if not reinforced.[1] If you decide to stop running completely after this program (but my prayer is that you continue to run long after you finish this study!), in just two short weeks you will begin to lose the muscular and cardiovascular endurance you gained while training.[2] In other words, as the old saying goes, "If you don't use it, you lose it." While calculated rest and recovery makes us stronger, when we stop running for significant periods of time we begin to lose any improvements we have gained.

I have experienced this myself. Just because I was able to run a 50K a couple of years ago doesn't mean I can run that distance now. Two years ago, I could run 20 miles one day and turn right around the next morning and run 10 more. If I attempted that right now, I would injure myself because I have not maintained that intense level of training.

If you think about it, the same can be said for almost any skill or ability. When weightlifters stop lifting all those weights, they quickly lose their muscle mass and strength. I studied French in high school and college and by the end of my fourth year of French, I was able to comprehend almost everything I read and heard. Now, my oldest is taking his first year of French, and when he asks me to help him with his homework I'm amazed at how much of my understanding of the language I have lost over the years.

Can you think of a skill or ability you once had, but have lost because you stopped using it? _____

_____

The only way to maintain our skills is to consistently, faithfully work at them—whether it's running, strength training, or a foreign language. But I do have good news, too! Although our fitness levels rapidly decrease with complete inactivity, if we maintain even a minimal fitness base—just a couple of days per week of running—we can regain our fitness levels quickly once we begin training again.

I may not be able to run a 50K right now, but because I have maintained a reasonable mileage base over the last couple of years I know that with consistent, progressive training I can get back to running 20 milers followed by 10 milers. In fact, I am counting on that because my big goal this year is to run a 50-mile trail race!

So what are we to do when injury or illness prevents us from being able to run? Tell most avid runners they can't run for a while and they are likely to fall into despair. Those of us who love running have the impression that the only way to maintain our fitness level is to run. So if we're faced with not being able to run, many of us will choose to stop exercising altogether; but a better choice would be to use this opportunity to try a different fitness plan.

Depending on your injury, you may be able to swim, cycle, or take a yoga class. Taking this time to stretch and strengthen will enhance your running once you are back on the road. While you may lose some of your running endurance, you may find a cross-training exercise you enjoy almost as much as running. When you're finally able to get back on the road, you'll find it is much easier to rebuild your running fitness if you haven't stopped exercising completely.

The worst thing we can do for our fitness is to quit. That sounds like something from our perseverance chapter, doesn't it? I find that as I dig deeply into the relationship between physical and spiritual training, one of the biggest keys to both is to just not stop!

What if we apply the reversibility principle to our spiritual lives? The parable of the talents is a perfect example of spiritual "use it or lose it." Read the parable Jesus tells his followers in Matthew 25:14-30 in order to answer the following questions:

How much money does the master give each of his servants?
Servant 1 _____
Servant 2 _____
Servant 3 _____

When the master returns, he asks each servant for an accounting of his money. How do the first two servants answer him, and what are their rewards?
Servant 1 _____

_____

_____

Servant 2 _____

_____

What did servant 3 do with his master's money, and how did his master receive this news? _____

_____

_____

Who does the master represent in this story? _____

The NLT Life Application Study Bible titles this parable "the parable of the *loaned* money"[3] (emphasis added). Dictionary.com defines *loan* as "the temporary use of something."[4] The master loaned his money to each of the servants, with the understanding that the money would be invested and returned to him.

The servants who were faithful with the money—investing it wisely so they were able to give back more than they received—were rewarded with more responsibility. The third servant didn't even deposit it in the bank, where at least he could have earned some interest. He simply buried it. Maybe he thought that since he was given less money than the other servants to start with, there was no reason to even bother. After all, he was only given one bag of money while the other two servants were given two bags and five bags.

Jesus tells us this parable to show us that each of us have been given certain abilities and talents to use to further God's Kingdom. It doesn't matter how big or small our gifts may seem compared to others. When we are faithful to use them to glorify God, our reward will be huge.

I've been guilty of being the third servant in this story. *I only have 30 minutes to exercise, so why even bother?* Yet it only takes two weeks of "why bother" and I have lost my cardiovascular and muscular endurance.

Or *I don't have anything special to give God. My days are spent running the kids around, grocery shopping, doing laundry...* I forget that even those daily tasks give me an opportunity to glorify God. I glorify Him when I have a heart that is grateful for those "mundane" tasks, when I recognize that everything I have is on loan from Him, and everything I do can be used for His glory.

Can you think of a time when you had a "why bother" attitude?

_____

_____

God delights in blessing us with more when we are faithful to what we have already been given. In fact, He *promises* blessing. While most of us consider blessing to be financial in nature, it goes way beyond earthly material possessions. In the Old Testament, earthly wealth certainly was an indicator of God's blessing. In the New Testament, though, the emphasis is on spiritual, eternal blessings.

According to Paul in Ephesians 1:3, how many blessings does God give us through Christ? _____

If he promises to bless us with *every* spiritual blessing, then let's take a look at just a few of those blessings. Underneath each blessing are verses that point to the promise of that blessing:

- A new heart, full of the Spirit: 2 Corinthians 1:21-22, Galatians 4:6
- Adoption into His Kingdom: Ephesians 1:5, Romans 8:14-16
- Forgiveness: Acts 13:38, Ephesians 1:7
- Hope: Colossians 1:22-23, Romans 5:1-6
- Love: Galatians 2:20, Galatians 5:22
- Patience: Romans 15:5, Colossians 1:11

To paraphrase Charles Spurgeon, although we are to give God thanks for all of our earthly blessings for they are far more than we deserve, the spiritual blessings we have in Christ are the rarest, richest, and the most enduring of all blessings. No temporal, earthly blessing can ever come close to the spiritual blessings we have in Christ.[5]

When we take the attitude of "why bother" or forget that every ability and blessing—the big and the small—are given to us by God to ultimately glorify His Kingdom, we lose sight of those precious spiritual blessings. Patience becomes frustration, peace turns to worry, and hearts become bitter and jaded.

The enemy loves it when we allow the reversibility principle to sneak into our spiritual walks. He capitalizes on it! He whispers to us: *God's blessings are out of reach; they are not meant for you, so you might as well just give up.*

Don't let him deceive you. We are heirs to the throne, adopted into His Kingdom. As such, His gifts are always available to us. To find them we need only to look up, to the One who gave us everything—including His only Son.

As we wrap up today's study, in the space below, write a prayer to God thanking Him for all the blessings you have—both spiritual and earthly. Ask Him to help you take those blessings and multiply them for His glory.

_____

_____

_____

_____

_____

Study Day 2

I am the true grapevine, and my Father is the gardener. He cuts off every branch of mine that doesn't produce fruit, and he prunes the branches that do bear fruit so they will produce even more.

John 15:1

Before we jump into today's study, let's review what we learned earlier this week. Can you remember the principle we discussed in Day 1?

_____

_____

How does this principle affect our physical and spiritual training?

_____

_____

_____

_____

I hope you had a chance to meditate on the promises we have in Christ because we are going to spend some more time discussing them today as we learn about the concept of **progressive overload**.

We have spent the last 10 weeks building a strong mileage base. As we discussed back in Week 2, a strong running foundation begins with mileage. In fact, doing speed work before you have a solid running base can lead to injury. At the end of this training, you will have a foundation of 10 miles! Did you ever think you would be able to say that?

One of my goals in this study is to give you the tools you need to continually mature as a runner and a Christian. Take a few minutes to review some of our previous chapters. What are some basics of running that you have put into practice?

_____

_____

_____

_____

The basics of running never change. Elite and novice runners alike require good shoes, core strength, proper form, good nutrition, and consistent training. Some of us have been running longer and have a stronger mileage base. Some of us run faster than others; and despite proper training, some of us may end up fighting injury. But if we want to keep running, we must put those shoes on and train. The same basic principles help elite and newbie runners alike grow into stronger runners.

My hope as your coach is that you will grow beyond the beginning runner. That as you grow as a runner, those concepts you didn't really understand before running become second nature. You'll know to keep an eye on the condition of your shoes, and when to replace them with another pair of high-quality running shoes. That you'll recognize that you are only as strong as your core. That rest and recovery are just as important as training.

What related basic spiritual concepts can we put into practice that will help us to mature in our faith?

_____

_____

_____

The basics of our Christian walk never change, no matter where we are in our faith walk. Whether we've just begun to know Jesus or have walked with Him for years, we all must consistently seek God, filling our hearts and minds with His Word. We must maintain strong core beliefs, keep soft hearts, and move forward in faith. But at some point we must move beyond the basics, both as runners and as Christians.

From this running base of 10 miles, you will be ready to choose a variety of different training programs. For example, you will be fully prepared for a 5K or 10K; but with a little bit more training, you will be ready to run an even faster half marathon and you will be over half of the way in training for a full marathon! Don't let this race be your last. Take this foundational mileage and build on it because each new challenge will make you a stronger runner.

So when do we reach our peak fitness? When can we rest in our training? Our running goals will dictate how far and fast we train. You certainly don't have to be able to run fast or far to be a strong runner, but so many runners get stuck in the comfort of their same route, same mileage, same races, and race goals. While running the same 3-mile route, at the same pace, day after day is certainly better than not running at all, the best thing we can do for our bodies is shake up our routine.

Think back to your very first 5-mile run. Do you remember how you felt afterward?

_____

_____

_____

Maybe you were able to write that you felt great and the five miles were no big deal. I, on the other hand, can remember being completely exhausted for the rest of the day. I think I even had to take a nap. My legs and arms ached for a couple of days. Now, many years later, a 5-mile run is one of my short runs. It doesn't even phase me. My muscles aren't sore. I am not in the least bit tired because my body has adapted to that five mile training.

Whenever we challenge our bodies to increased mileage or speed, we place new stresses on our bones, joints, muscles, connective tissues, and nervous system.[6] At first, our bodies are very inefficient at responding to these new demands and we may experience sore muscles and fatigue; but after a few training sessions, our bodies learn to adapt and grow stronger.

If I never progressed past that 5-mile run, my body would adapt to that mileage. I would burn fewer calories as my body became efficient and my muscles, bones, joints, and nervous system would cease to grow stronger. In order to continue to grow stronger as a runner, I have to train in a way that consistently challenges me. These challenges, or stressors, can be in the form of speed work, interval training, hill training, and additional mileage.

This is essentially the concept of overload: "exercising at a level which causes the body to make specific adaptations to function more efficiently."[7] However, there is a fine line between overloading and overtraining. We want our bodies to strengthen and adapt; not break down and get injured, which is why we must *progressively* overload our bodies, and allow for periods of rest.

No pain, no gain?

Although progressive overload is meant to stress our bodies gradually, it doesn't mean that we will never experience discomfort in our training. Dagney Scott says, "Discomfort is your body telling you that it is working hard to achieve the challenge you have set for it. This is progress. Although the old saying 'no pain, no gain' is exaggerated and misguided, it is true that you must stress your limits in order to expand them. If you are following the rules about gradually increasing your training distances and speed, then the discomfort you feel will be a normal part of the improvement process."[8]

When I worked at a specialty running store, whenever I fit someone for a new pair of running shoes, I always asked what sort of pain they experienced while running. My goal was to help minimize any unnecessary pain with proper shoes, socks, and arch supports, and to offer advice to avoid overtraining injuries; but sometimes people would come in with proper shoes and socks, doing well-planned training, and still complain of muscle pain. They wanted a quick and easy fix to the discomforts of running. They didn't seem to want to hear the truth: discomfort is a natural part of training.

One of the greatest things running has taught me is that experiencing a little bit of discomfort is okay. I've learned to run in the heat, rain, and cold. I have learned to run through blistered feet, black toenails, one toenail that falls off and grows back several times a year (yes, I know, gross—but it's just part of running when you run as much as I do!), sore leg muscles, sore back muscles, and sore arm muscles. *{Editor's note: When I first met with Corinne* *and her husband to discuss the book, I saw a sticker in the back window of their car: "Toenails are for sissies."}*

After some of my longer runs and tougher training sessions, I hurt! But I've learned that even though I may be sore, I can still go out and run the next day and I will survive. I know that at some point during my races the discomfort will be strong enough to make me want to quit, yet I am able to push through it. I have learned to listen to my body, and have gotten better at distinguishing between the discomfort of growing stronger and pain caused by an injury that needs to be addressed. I can tell you from a lot of experience that the results of running—physically, emotionally, and spiritually—far outweigh the discomfort.

I'm not saying that in order to become stronger runners we have to inflict significant pain on ourselves. What I am saying is to expect—and embrace!—the discomfort as we grow stronger.

Spiritual discomfort

Just as we become stronger runners when we gradually increase our mileage and pace, we become stronger Christians as we grow in our understanding of Christ and His Kingdom. When we are new in our faith it's natural that we're just beginning to understand the basics of Christian teachings; but that's not where God wants us to stay. In fact, the author of Hebrews admonishes those who don't grow past basic Christian teachings, "You have been believers so long now that you ought to be teaching others. Instead, you need someone to teach you again the basic things about God's word. You are like babies who need milk and cannot eat solid food. For someone who lives on milk is still an infant and doesn't know how to do what is right" (Hebrews 5:12-13).

Growing in our Christian faith doesn't happen accidentally. It requires the purposeful training of our consciences, our senses, our minds, and our bodies to distinguish between right and wrong.[9] As we continue reading Hebrews

5:14 and 6:1-3, we are reminded that we should be continually maturing in our faith. According to these verses, when we grow in our faith, what can we hope to understand more fully?

God wants us to grow beyond just consuming spiritual food to actually producing fruit. In John 15, we read the beautiful metaphor Jesus used to illustrate this. The disciples had just finished a rather unusual Passover supper with Jesus. First Jesus shocked them by washing their feet himself, then he declared that someone at that table would betray him, and he confused them further by telling them that he would soon be leaving! Perhaps he led them through a vineyard on the way to the garden of Gethsemane after their supper. Chuck Smith suggests that perhaps the clusters of grapes carved on the gates of the temple courts prompted Jesus' illustration as they made their way to the garden.[10]

I love that Jesus always knows just the right words and illustrations to make the most impact on his followers! The illustrations Jesus used in John 15 would have been very easy for the disciples to understand; vineyards were common and important in Jesus' day. Before we read John 15, though, let's spend a little time exploring a vineyard so we too can truly understand what Jesus is saying.

If you have ever visited a vineyard during harvest season, then you have seen the rows and rows of strong, gnarled trunks and vines covered with clusters of juicy grapes peaking out from under the dark green leaves. It is quite an undertaking to get the vines to this point, requiring year-round maintenance by a vinedresser. His job is to tend the grapevines so that at harvest time each branch produces the maximum amount of grapes the vines can thoroughly ripen.

Christy Mrozek says that as grapevine branches age they become brittle and stop producing fruit. During the winter, the vinedresser cuts the dead branches back to allow new branches to grow. In spring, he gently ties the new, young branches to wire fences because the branches cannot withstand the weight of the ripened fruit on their own. Toward summer, as the branches begin to bud, the vinedresser prunes the bud clusters. Left unpruned, the branches will produce too many fruit clusters and will not be able to ripen the large crop or sustain adequate growth. Pruning allows sunlight and airflow to penetrate to the core of the plant which encourages maximum grape production. The vinedresser also cuts away any seedlings or "suckers" that grow up around the base of the vine. If left unattended, they will compete with the vines producing fruit. Finally, in autumn, the grapes are ripe and ready for harvest; and the vinedresser tenderly plucks each cluster, taking care not to damage the branch so it can produce fruit another year.[11]

Now with that picture of a vineyard and the vinedresser in our minds, take a moment to read John 15:1-6. God is the vinedresser. His desire is to produce in us—the branches—abundant, sweet fruit. According to John 15, how do we bear fruit?

_____

_____

_____

Grape clusters can only grow when they remain attached to the vine. Who is the vine?

_____

Even if branches remain on the vine, what must the vinedresser do to make sure even more fruit grows?

_____

_____

According to the Encyclopedia Britannica, horticultural pruning is:

> the removal or reduction of parts of a plant, tree, or vine that are
> not requisite to growth or production, are no longer visually pleas-
> ing, or are injurious to the health or development of the plant...
> [P]runing enhances plant shape and flowering potential; new
> growth emerges from the bud or buds immediately below the
> pruning cut.[12]

In the flowerbeds at my house in Florida, I planted pentas, impatiens, lantana, and Mexican petunias of all colors. Unfortunately, I am not great at keeping up with my plants once I have planted them. Plants at my house have to be pretty hardy because I have a tendency to forget to water and fertilize them.

After a few weeks of growing wild, and no water or fertilizer to speak of, the plants look thin and leggy and stop blooming. The flowers wither and brown. So I pull out my gardening shears, cut off all the old flowers, and trim back the leggy stalks. I give them a healthy shower of water and sprinkle nutrients on the soil. My flower beds look pretty bare and colorless after I'm done pruning and feeding them, but just a few days later the weak, leggy stems begin to fill in with new, healthy leaves. Even more flowers bloom than the ones I cut off! Although I am not crazy about the actual pruning process, I am always glad I took the time because the results are abundant, full, colorful flowerbeds.

As we choose to remain in Christ, God lovingly prunes our lives. He doesn't want our spiritual lives to become old and brittle, incapable of producing more fruit. He carefully, lovingly cuts away those areas of our lives that hinder us from new growth. But He doesn't stop there...He prunes the buds of fruit on the new branches. You see, He doesn't just want *good* fruit, He wants the *best* fruit for our lives: His fruit. Then He gently ties those soft tender shoots to the support of the vine because He knows it is only when we remain tied to Christ, the Vine, that the fruit will ripen to its fullest potential.

Jesus promises that the fruit that will spring forth from our lives includes answered prayer, and lives filled with joy and love (John 15:7, 11-12). Peter also lists some of the virtues that will grow in our lives as we are lovingly pruned by our Father. According to 2 Peter 1:5-8, what are some of these characteristics?

_____

_____

_____

_____

These characteristics will grow and strengthen as God prunes our lives. Can you think of a time when you felt God pruning an area of your life in order to produce more of His fruit?

_____

_____

I've sure felt that, and let me tell you, some of that pruning was pretty painful. Just as I know I will hurt when I run hills, or increase my pace, God promises that our growth will not be without some pain. We've said that we must progressively overload our muscles, cardiovascular system, bones, and joints to force them to adapt and become more efficient. Our bodies then adapt to the new stressors placed on them and we once again progress to a harder workout. God knows that, in the same way, in order to grow spiritually, we must sometimes go through some discomfort.

Pain and stress bring accomplishment

For the last five years, my family has spent a week each winter skiing in the Rockies. I usually enrolled in at least one lesson each year to remind me of the basics, and then I spent the rest of the week skiing easy green-rated slopes. I am not fond of going fast, and I am even less fond of falling down! Since moving to Colorado, we have had the opportunity to ski almost every weekend; but until recently, I still wasn't comfortable skiing on anything but greens and maybe an easy blue, here and there.

My husband's childhood friend invited us to ski with her one weekend, and assured me that—being from Texas—she and her friends were going to stick to easier slopes. As we got off the lift at the top of the mountain, the group decided on an easy blue run. I nodded in agreement as my stomach churned and I thought, *Please let this truly be an "easy" blue!*

My heart pounded as I looked down at the steepest run I had ever attempted to ski. The group took off and I watched them gracefully and effortlessly ski down the mountain. I stood at the top of the run, petrified.

I slowly traversed across the mountainside, trying to remember all the things my ski instructors taught me. *Lean forward, knees over toes. Weight on downhill foot. Shift weight to turn.*

I stopped at one point to catch my breath and give my burning quads a rest. I looked back up the mountain and realized I had skied over halfway down! It was hard, but I was doing it—and I hadn't even come close to falling! With a little more confidence, I skied the rest of the way down to the group waiting at the bottom.

We spent the rest of the day skiing blues. I got faster and felt more confident with each hill. Toward the end of the day, my legs felt like jelly so I decided to go down an easier green to give my quads a break. I couldn't believe how easy the green was—almost boring! Yet the weekend before, this green was all I would have ventured to do if left on my own.

God pushes us outside our comfort zones in order to help us grow. He knows that in the discomfort there is growth. We learn that, with Him beside us, we are capable of so much more than we ever thought possible.

Abraham was stretched beyond the safety and comfort of his homeland to become the father of Israel. Moses was stretched to become a speaker and leader, leading God's people out of slavery. Esther was stretched to not only become a queen, but then confront her king for the sake of her people. Gideon was stretched to pare down his army of 33,000 men to an army of only 300 before leading them into battle.

Romans 5:3-6 tells us what growth can occur through our suffering. Write these verses in your own words:

_____

_____

_____

James tells us to "consider it pure joy, whenever you face trials of many kinds, because you know that the testing of your faith produces perseverance. Let perseverance finish its work so that you may be mature and complete, not lacking anything" (James 1:2-4).

I have to be honest: rejoicing and considering it pure joy is not always on my mind as I face discomfort and suffering. Sometimes I throw a great big pity party for myself; other times I get downright mad. More than once, I have found myself crying out to God, *Why me? This isn't fair!*

Can you think of a time when you threw a pity party for yourself while in the midst of suffering?

_____

_____

But how can we expect to go through life without enduring even just a portion of His suffering? Through our pain, we learn to adapt. We grow stronger in Him. We learn to remain in Him. We are able to encourage others as Jesus encourages us.

When we think we can no longer bear the discomfort and suffering, there is someone who has experienced more suffering than we can possibly imagine and who is willing to hold us up and help us through the pain. He may not take the pain away because He knows that through the pain, pruning, and cutting, there is growth; but He is there to comfort us through the pain. Jesus endured it all—the pain of betrayal by a friend, the pain of friends' denials, the pain of hatred, unfairness, being beaten, humiliated, being hung on a cross, spit at, and the pain of bearing all of our sin.

It comforts me to know that no suffering, no pruning is too big for Him to bear. As I move beyond the basics and grow into a more mature follower of Christ, I can look forward to the discomfort of God's pruning. Pruning, while painful, means growth with the reward of His fruit.

Take some time to reflect on that this week as you stretch yourself during your last 10-mile training run. Though your legs may ache and your lungs may burn, you are growing into a stronger runner. Your physical body will bear the fruit of your training with stronger muscles and improved endurance as we spend our final two weeks together.

Week 11

Part of a Community

After completing this week's training and homework you will:

- realize the dangers of comparison, in running and in life,
- recognize the need for accountability,
- have an understanding of the importance of encouragement, and
- see the value of relationship.

> *Share each other's burdens, and in this way obey the law of Christ.*
> *If you think you are too important to help someone,*
> *you are only fooling yourself. You are not that important.*
> *Pay careful attention to your own work, for then you will get the satisfaction of a*
> *job well done, and you won't need to compare yourself to anyone else.*
> Galatians 6:2-4

Welcome to our final week of training. Yes, we actually have two weeks remaining before our race, but this is the last week of training. Next week will be devoted to tapering our mileage and resting. Our long run this week is significantly shorter—only eight miles max—with two of those miles at race pace, so your body remembers what that feels like. If you have gotten at least two of the ten-mile training runs in, you can trust that you have enough mileage under your feet to run a half marathon. Another ten miler this week will only wear you out before your race, so enjoy your shorter run (did you ever think you would be able to say eight miles is a "short" run?) and savor your final week of training.

A word of caution: If you have missed a third or more of your training runs, you need to seriously consider whether you can comfortably complete 13.1 miles. If you were able to complete one of the ten mile training runs without excessive soreness and exhaustion, you should be able to complete the half marathon at an easy pace—but not at race pace. If ten miles was more than you could handle, you should consider skipping this race and finding another in a few weeks after you have had a chance to build up your mileage base. Remember, the great thing about running is there is always another race!

Last week we introduced a couple of new principles into our running and spiritual lives. As best as you can, write the definitions of them from memory (if you need help, go back to Week 10.)

Reversibility Principle _____

_____

_____

Progressive Overload _____

_____

_____

Hopefully last week encouraged you to continue your training beyond this study—especially now that the end is in sight!

Week 11 TRAINING SCHEDULE

There are 5 workouts (4 runs, 1 cross training) and 2 rest days each week.
The workout days are flexible, however use 1 rest day after your longest run.

WEEK 11	WORKOUT 1	WORKOUT 2	WORKOUT 3	WORKOUT 4	WORKOUT 5	WORKOUT 6	WORKOUT 7
PLAN	Easy Run 50-60 min OR Easy Pace 10 Race Pace 30 Easy Pace 10	X-train 30 min + 20 min core	Easy Run 35 min (spend 10 min on form)	Easy Run 45-55 min + 10 min core	Rest	Long Run 8 miles (in miles 5-6 run at Race Pace)	Rest
LOG							

Always spend 5-10 minutes warming up and 5-10 minutes cooling down. This can be included in your total time/mileage.

Long Run: These should be at an easy, conversational pace.
Easy Run: Easy runs should be at an easy, conversational pace. On a scale of 1-10 (10 being all out effort), an easy run should feel like a 5-6.
Race Pace: The pace you plan to run during your race as predicted on page 135.
X-train: Cross-training. Anything other than running, such as swimming, biking, walking, strength training.
LOG: This is where you write what you ACTUALLY did that day, along with a description of how you prepared and how you felt.
Core: Choose a few core exercises and spend time strengthening your core after your run.
Form: Concentrate on your running form during your run. Arms, neck, foot placement, breathing...

For just as each of us has one body with many members, and these members do not all have the same function, so in Christ we, though many, form one body, and each member belongs to all the others. — ROMANS 12:4-5 (NIV)

(This page is left blank so that you can cut out the workout plan on the other side and display it where you'll see it regularly.)

Study Day One

The past few weeks have been spent discussing topics that focus on our individual running and spiritual lives. This week we are going to look beyond ourselves at the large race community we're part of.

The popularity of the half marathon has exploded over the last decade. Since 2003, the half marathon has been the fastest growing race distance in the US, growing over 10% each year. In 2009, 1.1 million people finished a half marathon![1]

Why do I tell you this? To help you get a feeling for the enormous half marathon race community. Over one million men and women of different ethnicities, ages, backgrounds, sizes, and shapes. Over one million different training programs, struggles, and stories with the same ultimate goal: to cross the finish line.

Because half marathons have become so popular, many of them now use race start corrals, or waves, to efficiently get people over the start line and help ease congestion on the racecourse over the first couple of miles. The corrals are usually divided by pace per mile, so when you reach your race's start area look for the corral that most closely matches what you plan to race. Some large races will assign you a start corral and print it on your race number patch. Smaller races will simply announce that faster runners should move toward the front, and slower runners toward the back. If this is your first race, plan to start near the back so you don't accidentally get in the way of those trying to set PR's.

Picking the right start corral is a good way to maintain the race pace you have targeted, since the people around you will be going the same speed.

Don't feel like starting near the back is somehow negative. My favorite place to hang out before a race is toward the back, with the first-time racers and slower runners. I love to hear their stories of how they started running, and the struggles they went through to get to the race start. I really appreciate the opportunity to encourage them on their race journey. The atmosphere is usually inviting and uplifting, with each person hoping to have not only a good race themselves, but wishing those around them their best race as well.

I remember standing at the start of one race, where I accidentally ended up in a start corral a little faster than my goal pace. The air was competitive, as each runner silently sized up the runners nearby. The only conversations were about how fast they had been in previous races, how many miles a week they run on average, and how fast they were going to run this race. I felt indignant eyes staring at me, as if to say, "You don't belong here. You don't look fast enough to be standing with us." I even heard a couple of calculated remarks about how it was so annoying to have to run around slow runners who had picked a race start that was too fast.

Have you ever been in a group where you felt as though you didn't belong? That somehow you didn't measure up? Write your experience and how it made you feel:

_____

_____

_____

_____

_____

_____

What's sad is that I probably could have held my own in this group. Perhaps, with some encouragement, I could have had the race of my life as this group held me to a tougher pace. Instead, feeling unwelcomed and judged, I quietly edged my way backward to the slower paced runners.

I understand the reasons behind having faster runners at the front and slower runners at the back of the start of a race. It creates a safer racecourse and helps the flow of racers, which at the start can be quite congested. That's why the larger races have corral starts based on pace and finish time, and why it's important to do your best to start in the corral that fits your pace.

But why do some feel it is okay to project an air of elitism, as though performance is the only way to judge one's running worthiness? Why would some go out of their way to make runners feel unwelcome? The runners in that faster pace corral judged me without even getting to know me.

I have encountered running clubs with this same attitude. There are clubs whose members are unwelcoming to anyone new, and whose only metric for running is a fast pace and high weekly mileage. As you get stronger and faster, never forget the insecurity of your first race. Be sure to encourage others the way you wanted to be encouraged.

Have we forgotten the Golden Rule?

I recently heard a story about a woman who showed up at a running club's weekly group run. She was new to running, and on this wintry evening she came dressed in bulky cotton sweatpants and a knee-length down jacket. The seasoned runners in the group snickered at her clothing, and did absolutely nothing to make her feel welcome. They didn't bother to introduce themselves, or to take the time to find out anything about this woman—who had probably been nervous and unsure about even showing up. She disappeared before the run was even over. If that had been me, I probably would have given up running altogether.

It seems that some seasoned, talented runners sometimes forget that they, too, were once beginning runners. Veteran runners should encourage, uplift, and educate beginners! There's enough room on the racecourse for all of us—beginners, veterans, the speedy, and the plodders.

Encountering runners with self-righteous attitudes who base another runner's worth on their own definition of performance brings back all of the doubts about my abilities as a runner. As a beginning runner, I had so many self-defeating thoughts running through my head:

- I'm not really a runner
- I'm not fast enough
- I don't run enough miles to be considered a real runner
- I don't belong in this group
- I will never measure up

On your running journey have you had any of these same thoughts? Circle any of my thoughts that you have shared, and below write any other self-defeating thoughts you may have:

_____

_____

_____

_____

_____

Do you see a pattern? Those thoughts come from a perspective of comparison! When I compare myself to faster runners, or runners who are able to run more miles than me, I feel like I don't measure up. But if I turn it around and compare myself to slower, or beginning runners, then I risk becoming self-righteous myself, thinking I am better.

We are runners—regardless of our pace or weekly mileage—because we train to run. We set goals and strive to reach those goals. Sometimes we fail, sometimes we get injured, and sometimes we set a new PR.

We all have different strengths and weaknesses. Some of us are great at endurance. Others may be great at picking up the pace at the end. Still others may thrive on hills. We each have different maximum heart rates and fueling requirements. For some running is natural and easy, while for others it is work!

We have our own struggles, mental and physical, that we have overcome to get to the starting line of our race. Comparing ourselves to those around us serves no positive purpose.

If comparing ourselves with other runners can make us feel inferior or self-righteous, how much more dangerous is comparison on our Christian walk? It is so easy to look at those around us and think we don't measure up in some way. Think about some of the ways we compare ourselves to others and end up feeling inferior:

- finances
- spiritual maturity
- _____
- _____
- _____
- _____
- _____

In what ways might we think that we are better off than others? (You may find some of the above answers work here too!)

- _____
- _____
- _____
- _____

Now circle any of those answers that have personally been struggles for you.

Lest we think we're the only ones who struggle with comparison, turn to John 21:15-22 and read how even the disciples struggled at times too. Jesus has just finished asking Peter—not once, but three times—if he loves Jesus. Jesus then tells Peter to follow Him, even though it will most likely result in Peter's own death.

What does Peter ask Jesus about John (the one who was following them as they had this conversation) in John 21:21?

_____

_____

How many times have you been guilty of asking God that same question? How often have you compared your situation, your calling, your gifts, your struggles to those around you and asking God *"Well, what about her? What about him?"* How does Jesus respond to Peter's question?

_____

_____

Jesus doesn't offer explanation as to why Peter's fate is different than John's. He simply says "What is that to you?"

Jesus is in essence telling Peter: *Don't worry about John's race. John's pace and John's finish are not your concern. You concentrate on your own race. Follow me and concentrate on your own race. I will get you to your finish line in my perfect timing.*

Kristin Armstrong, runner and author, says:

> God gives us all different gifts. If you are so busy looking at what your neighbor got, you will miss the gifts you have been given. By comparing yourself to others you cease to be grateful for what you have, because you are focusing on what you don't have. By coveting your neighbor's life, you are not living your own. Keep your eyes straight ahead. You must run your own race.[2]

When we compare ourselves to others, we take our focus off Christ. Instead of comparing, we are called to encourage and hold each other accountable. Besides, we're often good at giving the impression that we have things more together than we really do—you're probably comparing yourself to an incorrect perception of that other person anyway!

Community builds accountability

One of the reasons I love training with a group is the accountability. Knowing there is a group of people waiting for me forces me out of my warm, cozy bed early on a Saturday morning. And once I'm out of bed and running, there have been so many times that I would have quit from fatigue had it not been for those running alongside me, holding me to my goal for the day. My running groups hold me to my training plan. My beginning runners remind me of how important the basics are, and my advanced runners push me to continually learn.

When we run as a group we're able to push each other through our speed work session, or force each other to slow down during an easy run. Group runs give all of us—beginner and veteran alike—the opportunity to share life with each other. Some of my best spiritual conversations have been shared in a group training run. There is something about sweating together, hearts racing and muscles aching, that lends itself to honesty and vulnerability. Defenses break down and walls crumble after a few miles. It's Christian fellowship at its best—what Paul calls us to in Galatians 6:1-4.

According to Paul, we are to _____ our brothers and sisters in Christ, taking care not to _____ ourselves (v. 1). We should carry each other's _____ (v. 2), and not think we are too _____ to help someone else (v. 3). Rather than compare ourselves to those around us, our satisfaction should come from _____ (v. 4), looking to Christ as our example. Paul goes on to say that we should "do good to everyone—especially to those in the family of faith" (v. 10).

Who knows, maybe our encouragement will be what fuels our brothers and sisters to cross their finish line. I'll never forget the silent encouragement offered to me in the last three miles of a race. In an attempt at a PR, I was running hard. Every muscle burned, and my brain was trying to convince my legs that it was time to slow down. I was about to give in when I felt someone running just behind me. I glanced behind me and saw a woman I had chatted with at the start corral. I could tell she was laboring as hard as I was.

Without a word—neither of us could afford to waste energy speaking—our strides matched and we ran side by side. If I pulled ahead, she matched my pace. If she pulled ahead I matched hers. As we rounded the corner and saw the finish line ahead, maybe half a mile away, the pain in my muscles was more than I could bear. I felt my pace weaken. Now she was two or three steps ahead of me. Noticing that I was no longer next to her, she glanced back and spoke for the first time.

"Don't you let me beat you!"

Somehow I mustered energy I didn't think I had, and I caught back up. Our pace quickened and we ran strong to the finish, both of us giving it everything we had. We crossed the finish line together and collapsed into each other's arms, hugging each other, tears filling our eyes. I told her I couldn't have finished the race without her. She was my motivation to keep running strong.

"Me?" She exclaimed. "The only reason I finished was because of you!"

To this day I don't know this woman's name. Our lives intertwined for only three short miles, but in that time we each encouraged the other to run strong to the end. Think about an instance when someone encouraged you. How did the encouragement help you through a tough time?

_____

_____

_____

_____

When we encourage others, we help them run their own races to the best of their abilities. We can't run someone else's race. The lady who ran beside me didn't stop running her race when I slowed. She knew she had to finish her race with or without me—but she did her absolute best to encourage me to stay with her.

We can't train for others and we can't force them to move their feet. But we can offer encouragement and be there beside them to lift them up as they struggle to take the next step.

Encouraging God's plan for others

Moses was forbidden to enter the Promised Land. After freeing the Israelites and leading them through the desert for forty years, he could only gaze upon the Promised Land from afar. Instead of entering the Promised Land, what does Deuteronomy 3:28 say he was to do?

_____

_____

Can you imagine being told that not only are you not allowed to enter the land you've spent forty years of your life trying to get to, but that you have to train up and encourage the person who is going to take your place? I have to be honest, I probably would have harbored a bit of resentment towards Joshua. But Moses, in obedience to God, diligently spent the rest of his days preparing the Israelites, writing down the laws of God, and raising up Joshua to become the next leader.

In front of the nation of Israel, Moses announced Joshua would be their new leader. How did Moses encourage and lift Joshua up in front of the entire nation (Deuteronomy 31:7-8)? _____

_____

_____

You know your heart is in the right place when you want success for God's purpose and not to puff up your own pride. This is what Paul meant when he said "So I have reason to be enthusiastic about all Christ Jesus has done through me in my service to God. Yet I dare not boast about anything except what Christ has done through me" (Romans 15:17-18).

After Paul's Damascus Road experience he spent the rest of his life encouraging Christians to live out their faith. Although he wasn't afraid to admonish when necessary, he also knew the power of encouragement. Let's take a tour of Paul's ministry and write down some of the uplifting words Paul spoke and wrote to his fellow believers.

Paul wrote to the Christians in Rome for many reasons—to inform them of his upcoming visit, to define faith and present God's plan of salvation, and to implore the Roman Jews and Gentiles to live in harmony. But before he tackled these topics, he opened his letter with this encouragement:

Romans 1:8-12 _____

_____

_____

_____

About the same time that he wrote Romans, Paul wrote 2 Corinthians to defend his ministry, which was being discredited by false teachers. The church of Corinth itself was divided and rife with controversy. Yet, even within such a strongly worded letter, Paul took the time to encourage the believers:

2 Corinthians 7:4_____

_____

Although the Thessalonians were progressing as a church they had fallen prey to false doctrine. Paul knew he had to clear up these false teachings and fast, so he wrote 2 Thessalonians. But again, Paul knew that along with the truth, the new believers needed encouragement in their faith:

2 Thessalonians 1: 3-4 _____

_____

Paul's words teach us the importance of encouraging one another in truth and love, even through our struggles, our sins, and our triumphs. With our eyes focused on our own race, we have the freedom to uplift and encourage those beside us who are running their own races. Our words and actions have the power to help someone cross their finish line strong!

Study Day Two

For just as each of us has one body with many members, and these members do not all have the same function, so in Christ we, though many, form one body, and each member belongs to all the others.
Romans 12:4-5 (NIV)

I hope you had a chance this week to offer encouragement to someone in his or her life's race. Today we're going to continue on the topic of community by taking a look at the actual race itself.

There is an entire community of people who come together to put on a race, and the runners are just one part. Organizing even a small race is a huge undertaking. The race director and staff–many of whom volunteer their time while maintaining regular full-time jobs—spend countless hours organizing the race event. Each detail must come together, from runner registration to ordering t-shirts and medals, stuffing goody bags, measuring and marking the course, hiring the company to time the runners, organizing the volunteers, ordering the drinks, applying for city permits to close down the streets, and organizing the post-race party. And that's just a partial list of all the tasks!

Once race day finally arrives, volunteers who have been up since dawn spend hours handing out water and sports drinks, cleaning up streets filled with discarded cups, and putting medals on sweaty, exhausted runners. Police officers, usually working overtime, stand at busy intersections to direct traffic so the runners don't have to stop running. Medics are on hand to help runners who have become injured or ill. And we can't forget the spectators, standing on the streets for hours, cheering on the runners as they run by. Each part is vital to the success of the race.

> *I encourage runners to volunteer for races they don't plan to run, in order to experience a race from another perspective and to see first hand just how important each volunteer is to the overall race process.*

Part of the excitement of participating in a race is being able to interact with all of those different people who have come together to ensure that the race will be a success. It saddens me to see more and more runners diminishing their race experience by shoving earbuds in their ears at the start, spending the entire race in their own little worlds. They miss the cheering, the interaction with runners around them, the words of encouragement, and the atmosphere of celebration. On a practical level, not being able to hear race instructions and others around you can be hazardous. Several years ago the United Sates Track and Field Association, the governing body for road races, actually banned the use of headphones during races. Due to the challenge of enforcing the rule, though, the USATF amended the rule in 2008 to allow each individual race director the option to allow headphones.[3] You will want to check the rules of each race you enter to determine whether you can wear headphones.

While I won't tell anyone to never listen to music during a race, I do have a few suggestions:

- Avoid wearing earbuds when the racecourse is crowded. It is important to be able to hear the runners around you to avoid accidentally tripping someone. One misstep in a crowded race and many people can stumble and get hurt. Once the course thins out it is safer to listen to music.

- Take your earbuds out when you come to a water station. This way you can hear any race announcements. You can hear the volunteers calling out what type of drink they have in their hands, so you'll know which table has sports drinks and which table has water. You can also say a sincere "thank you" to them for volunteering. Remember, everyone can use encouragement!

- Take your earbuds out as you get close to the finish line. You will need to hear any finish-line instructions. One lady didn't hear the instructions being called out and she crossed the marathon finish line instead of the half-marathon finish line. After all her hard work, her official result was a DNF. Besides, why would you want to miss the cheer of the crowd as you race to the finish? That's as inspirational as any song!

- If you do listen to music, you must pay attention to your surroundings. I learned this the hard way! While listening to music and not paying attention, I once missed the split where the half and full marathons separated. I had to double back to get on the correct course, which cost me some time—and was a little embarrassing.

The actions you take in your race effects those around you. Stopping suddenly in the middle of the course to retie your shoe can inadvertently cause the runners behind you to stumble. Throwing your sports drink cup with no regard for where it will land might douse another runner's legs and feet with sticky liquid causing their skin to blister and chafe. Changing directions without first looking behind you might cause another runner to trip.

I don't want to be the reason another runner's race is less than what they had hoped for. Of course, accidents do happen. In a crowded race as I attempted to cross over to a water table I accidentally collided with another runner—and I mean full-force! I almost knocked myself over. Luckily (for him, anyway) he was much bigger than me, so the collision hurt me worse than it did him.

He was a very good sport about it and we ended up running together for a few minutes, but I have seen others who haven't fared as well. One lady was knocked to the ground as a guy—oblivious to his surroundings—cut her off. She was so injured she had to quit the race.

Don't forget that as a Christian runner, you are being held to a higher standard. Non-believers are watching you! They are listening to your comments and watching your behavior. While it's true that we all fall short and make mistakes, let's do our best to race in a Christ-like way—helping others finish their races, not causing them to stumble physically or spiritually.

We will go over race day do's and don'ts as well as race etiquette in week 12, so you will be fully prepared for your race. Don't let the above scare you into never attempting a race. The key is maintaining a sense of awareness and to actively participate in the race!

Living in isolation

If you think about it, our society has subtly and gradually moved away from interaction and relationship—from earbuds blocking out the race around us to drive-through windows at banks and restaurants so we don't even have to get out of our vehicles. The Internet lets us shop without ever leaving our living rooms, and e-mail and texts are often the preferred communication choice. As a result, human relationships have suffered. Don't get me wrong, I enjoy the convenience of Internet shopping and texting. But the enemy has done a pretty good job of separating us from each other, deceiving us into thinking we don't need relationship; that we can survive just fine in a world of minimal human interaction.

Think about your day-to-day life. List some of the ways your own life has evolved to decrease direct interaction with others: _____

_____

_____

_____

With the loss of relationship comes the loss of accountability and encouragement. Behind the anonymity of the Internet, our cars, and our cell phones, it is easy to act without regard for the consequences of our actions or the feelings of others.

Without relationship with our Creator and each other, we forget that we are called to love one another as Christ loved us. To "always be humble and gentle. Be patient with each other, making allowance for each other's faults because of your love" (Ephesians 4:2).

God created us to crave relationship—first and foremost with Him, but with others as well. He knew from the beginning we weren't meant to run our race alone, which is why He created Eve for Adam.

Jesus' ministry here on earth was one of relationships. He shared his life with his disciples, the needy, and the sinful. Although He knew the importance of spending one on one time with His Father, he also knew the value of sharing His life with those around Him. He knew that each person was valuable to God and His kingdom.

Each of us has a role in God's plan. God blesses each of us with unique gifts to use for His Kingdom. No one is more important than another, and God doesn't love one gift over another. With Christ as the head, "He makes the whole body fit together perfectly. As each part does its own special work, it helps the other parts grow, so that the whole body is healthy and growing and full of love" (Ephesians 4:16).

Read Romans 12:3-13. I love how Paul explains how each of us has a role in the Kingdom of God. According to Romans 12:4-5, how do they all work together?

_____

_____

_____

Just as a race can't function properly without the volunteers, medics, police—oh, and runners—we as Christians need each other to fully function under Christ! We need people to lean on as we navigate life's struggles. We need to love each other earnestly, and be there to help out when people are in trouble. (Romans 12:10, 13)

I have a handful of girlfriends who—no matter how much time has passed, no matter how much we have allowed life to get in the way of our relationships—I know I can call on them and they will instantly be at my side. In my struggles, they empathize and lift me up. In my triumphs, they shout for joy without jealousy. Through my relationships with these women I feel the love of Christ. Through them I am able to catch just a glimpse of His perfect Kingdom and his infinite love.

I can "do life" with these women. They have seen me with puffy eyes, a bright red nose, and splotchy face without makeup. They don't judge me when I admit my sin, but they're also not afraid to speak God's truth to me—even when I may not want to hear it. We walk out Romans 12 through our relationship. I treasure these women and thank God for them.

Do you have a friend or friends you can count on in a similar way? If you do, lift them up in prayer right now and thank God for them. If you have not yet found a friend like this, ask God to put someone in your life with whom you can share your Christian walk.

As we come to the last week of our time together, I truly hope that through this experience you have connected with at least one brother or sister in

Christ. Someone you can share your race with, sweat with, and set goals with. Someone who will hold you accountable and offer the encouragement you need to take just one more step. I am so very proud of your commitment and perseverance through this training program, and I'm honored to have had the chance to share it with you. You're on the home stretch and I can't wait to see what God has in store for you as we count down to our race day and beyond!

Week 12

Final Preparations

After completing this week's training and homework, you will:

- be rested and ready for your half marathon race,
- understand tapering, and
- know how to prepare for race day.

No, dear brothers and sisters, I have not achieved it, but I focus on this one thing: Forgetting the past and looking forward to what lies ahead, I press on to reach the end of the race and receive the heavenly prize for which God, through Christ Jesus, is calling us.
Philippians 3:13-14

Congratulations! You are here—the final week of training. I cannot begin to tell you how very proud I am of you. As I write, I am filled with such a mix of emotions—thrilled that you are just a few days away from your race, excited to see your hard work be put to the test on the race course, and sad that we are almost at the end of this training program!

Throughout this process, my prayer has been that you will be inspired to continue training—both physically and spiritually—for the rest of your life.

You have worked so hard to get here; don't allow it to just slip away. Whether you decide to continue to run or not, I hope that you have seen the benefits of training goals and of staying physically fit. Let this training program be a jumping off point to bigger and better things!

Take it easy!

Your training this week consists of **tapering**. Tapering is when you reduce your weekly training in order to allow your body to rest up and refuel for an upcoming race. Typically, a one-week taper (a shorter "long" run and less mileage overall the week of the race) is sufficient for a half marathon race.

While I usually welcome the restful week before a race, some runners find they feel antsy. They worry they are going to lose all of their hard training if they rest. Others get concerned that they haven't trained enough and should train hard right up to race day. *You have to resist the urge* to get in that last long run or to try to cram in those training runs you may have missed. The best you can do for yourself is to get extra sleep and allow your body to rest. Successful training programs reduce mileage—but not intensity—the week or two leading up to race day. Studies prove that proper tapering brings improved race performance … so relax and enjoy a week of fewer miles.[1]

With that said, if you look at your training schedule, you will notice that this week still involves *some* training. Our mileage decreases, but our intensity won't. If we taper too drastically, our bodies may relax so much that we end up feeling sluggish on race day—or worse, with the sniffles. So a couple runs at race pace will help us show up at the race start rested and ready.

So, instead of extra pavement pounding this week, let's focus on race preparation and the do's and don'ts of race week. This week, we won't have study days and homework—the spiritual side is mixed in with the other preparations—so I would like you to read through this entire chapter twice and practice the mental exercises daily. This will help you know what's com-

Week 12 TRAINING SCHEDULE _____

There are 5 workouts (4 runs, 1 cross training) and 2 rest days each week.
The workout days are flexible, however use 1 rest day after your longest run.

WEEK 12	WORKOUT 1	WORKOUT 2	WORKOUT 3	WORKOUT 4	WORKOUT 5	WORKOUT 6	WORKOUT 7
PLAN	Easy Run 40 min OR Easy Pace 10 Race Pace 20 Easy Pace 10	Rest OR Walk 30 min	Easy Run 35 min (spend 10 min on form)	Easy Run 35 min OR Easy Pace 10 Race Pace 15 Easy Pace 10	Rest	Race 13.1 miles!	Rest
LOG							

Always spend 5-10 minutes warming up and 5-10 minutes cooling down. This can be included in your total time/mileage.

Long Run: These should be at an easy, conversational pace.
Easy Run: Easy runs should be at an easy, conversational pace. On a scale of 1-10 (10 being all out effort), an easy run should feel like a 5-6.
Race Pace: The pace you plan to run during your race as predicted on page 135.
Form: Concentrate on your running form during your run. Arms, neck, foot placement, breathing...

No, dear brothers and sisters, I have not achieved it, but I focus on this one thing: Forgetting the past and looking forward to what lies ahead, I press on to reach the end of the race and receive the heavenly prize for which God, through Christ Jesus, is calling us. — PHILIPPIANS 3:13-15

(This page is left blank so that you can cut out the workout plan on the other side and display it where you'll see it regularly.)

ing, make sure you don't miss any information that is key to your race, and help you arrive at race day mentally strong and relaxed.

I love the week of a race! It's a relief knowing I have done all the training and am finally preparing for the actual race. The anticipation is so exciting! This chapter is going to be laid out chronologically, with tips for the whole week first and then additional information as we get closer to race day.

My preparation tips

I'm going to lay out a lot of tips this week, based on my experience from lots of races at a wide variety of venues. Please don't panic at the long lists! Not every rule will apply to every race. I'm just trying to cover as many situations as possible. Race preparation is really quite simple and involves a lot of common sense—but there are a few tips that you just don't know unless you are told (or in my case, unless you learn the hard way). I'd like to help you avoid some of the many mistakes I've made in my races. *Remember as you prepare this week to remain flexible. Focus on the things you can control, and don't worry about the things you can't control.*

The week leading up to the race

DO:

☺ Get extra sleep. The night before the race you probably won't get much. You'll be excited and nervous, and you'll need to get up early on race day; so get plenty of sleep in the days leading up to the race. If you can, take naps during the days.

☺ Trim and/or file your toenails 5-7 days before the race. That gives your toes time to get used to the shorter nails—plus a few days to grow, in case you accidentally cut one too short.

☺ Sip on water all week. A few sips of water every hour is better than one or two huge glasses all at once because your body can only absorb so much at one time. If you drink more than you can absorb, all it will accomplish is multiple trips to the bathroom.

☺ Download a race pace bracelet to help you stay on your race pace. A race pace bracelet gives you time splits for each mile, helping you determine if you are running too fast or not fast enough for your pace goal. There are several places online where you can create one, including marathonguide. com/fitnesscalcs/PaceBandCreator.cfm. Put tape on the entire backside of your bracelet first (that will help protect it from perspiration), then cover the front with tape to protect it from both perspiration and rain.

☺ Figure out what you are going to wear on race day and make sure it is all clean and packed. Your shoes, socks, and clothes should all be something you have run in before. Race day is not the time to try a new pair of shoes or socks or running clothes. I once ran a half marathon with a girl who tried a new running bra that zipped up the front. She bought it at the race expo (we'll talk about those later in the week) and was so excited to try it out that she decided to wear it for the first time in her race. By mile 10, the zipper had caused so much chafing that she was bleeding and miserable.

☺ Inspect your running shoes, inside and out. Pick out any pebbles that have gotten lodged in the tread of your shoes. Take out the sock liners (the removable insole inside your shoe) and arch supports, and dump any dirt or sand that may have accumulated during your runs.

☺ Make sure you have plenty of gels, chews, or whatever you have decided you will refuel with during the race. Race day is not the time to discover you are out of your favorite flavor.

☺ Take some time to go over your race's rules, instructions, and course map a few times during the week. The more prepared you feel about the racecourse and procedures, the less nervous you will be on race day.

☺ Check the weather forecast a couple of days before the race. Races do not get postponed for weather! If it looks like it might rain, pack a large garbage bag (yard-waste size) to use as rain gear at the race start. Cut out a hole for your head and arms. If the weather will be cool at the start, wear "throw away" clothes at the start. Throw away clothes are sweat pants, sweat shirts, gloves, and warm hats that you don't mind throwing on the side of the road as you warm up during the race. If you don't have any old clothes to throw away on the racecourse, go to your local drugstore or discount store and buy inexpensive sweat suits and gloves. You'll be so glad you did as you watch those around you shiver in their shorts and tank tops, waiting for the sun to come up on race morning. At one race where the temperature was below freezing and I knew I would be standing at the start for hours, I brought an old throw blanket to wrap around me and then tossed it along the side of the start corral when the race started. The clothes you toss on the side of the road are usually picked up by race volunteers and donated to charity. *TIP: Buy an inexpensive pair of knee socks or tube socks, cut the tip of the toes off, cut a hole for your thumb, and you have a terrific arm warmer that you can easily toss off to the side as you warm up.*

☺ Go over your race plan. Go back to Week 7 and reread your pace and performance goals, your race strategies, and what associative and dissociative strategies you will use during your race. Rewrite them below to help you remember—or if you have tweaked them since then, enter the new values:

My Mantra: _____

My Pace Goals: #1 _____

                 #2 _____

                 #3 _____

My Performance Goal(s): _____

_____

My Race Pace: _____

☺ If your plan is to simply finish the race (and there's nothing wrong with that in your first race!), you can use your first mile as a warm-up mile. Gradually increase your pace until by about mile one you are at your race pace.

☺ If you have a specific target finish time, you will want to spend a few minutes before the race warming up your muscles with either a few minutes of running (if that is possible) or some dynamic stretches. Honestly, it can be difficult to get a good warm up before a race, so don't worry about it too much. Aim to get within 10-20 seconds of your race pace in the first mile. You'll be able to make up that little bit of time in the later miles. Remember that starting out too fast will only cause you to hit the wall. Your best bet is to run at an even pace from start to finish.

☺ The time on the race clocks along the course track the *official* start time, which is not necessarily when *you* crossed the starting line. There have been larger races with multiple starts where I crossed the start line as much as fifteen minutes after the official start time! (Don't worry, that's why you will be given an individual timing chip.) It's best to wear a stopwatch, starting your time the moment you cross the start line. If you don't wear a watch, you will need to remember the time on the clock when you crossed the line and subtract that time from the official time.

☺ Set aside some time each day for mental preparation: Picture yourself at key points in the race, feel how your body will feel, and see yourself breaking through with determination. The more you do this, the more easily you will keep your confidence and strength when doubts and aches try to creep in.

☺ This is also why a daily time of prayer and meditation is so important. When life sends problems and doubts our way, we gain strength from the time we have spent with God. We gain confidence from knowing that we aren't facing any of these things on our own. He is with us, ready to give us loving support whenever we call.

☺ Look back over your running journal. It's okay to smile a little when you see a complaint you wrote about the challenge of running five miles for the first time. Now you've run 10 miles—and more than once! Look at how you've persevered and grown. Give yourself credit for how far you've come. Let it sink in that you really, truly are ready for this race.

☺ Likewise, this is the value of a spiritual journal—this week and for the rest of your life. Look how far you've come! The things in your journal from times past may look a bit immature to you now. Things that would have challenged your faith in the past are no longer a big deal. Celebrate the fact that God continues to allow you nearer and nearer to Him as you walk together. And remember: many of the people around you are where you used to be. That should help you look at them with love and grace, knowing that we're all on the same journey. You may be a little further along, but you were where they are; and the truth is that there are people farther along than you, so humility is always appropriate.

DON'T:

☹ Don't do any strength training this week. You want your muscles rested for the race. I once made the mistake of thinking I would just train my upper body a couple of days before a half marathon because only my legs needed to be rested. Huge mistake. My arms and core were so sore from my upper body workout that I could barely straighten my elbows or even take a deep breath. I was in serious pain during the entire race. Now, I allow myself to take the week off from all strength training so that I show up to the start line with relaxed, rested, pain-free muscles. If you *absolutely must* do a few core exercises, fine. Just keep them low-key and relaxed, and do ones that you already do on a regular basis. This week is not the week to try a new exercise routine!

☹ Don't get a pedicure this week. You can paint your toenails, if you like; but don't let anyone file down your hard-earned calluses. Tender, soft feet on race day lead to blisters and hot spots.

☹ Don't eat any new, unusual foods, especially the closer you get to race day. Now is not the time to try out that new Thai or Mexican restaurant. The last thing you need this week is an upset stomach from spicy foods! Instead, eat a balanced diet of lean, quality proteins, and fruits and veggies. You may indulge in a few extra high-carb foods leading up to race day, such as pasta, breads, rice, and potatoes, just to make sure your glycogen stores are topped off and ready for race day. Note: If you have blood sugar issues, consult your doctor about your diet before adding extra carbs.

☹ Don't worry if you gain a couple of pounds this week. Carbohydrates are stored with water, so as you eat plenty of carbs, you will probably gain some water weight. You will lose this naturally in the weeks after the race. Although I may weigh myself before and after a race just to keep track of my hydration, I don't worry if I'm a little heavier. I almost always weigh more than usual the week before and after a race as my body stores up carbs.

Three days before the race

If you are traveling out of town to your race, give yourself time to get to your destination without feeling stressed and pressed for time. If your race is in a different time zone or at a higher elevation, be sure to arrive a couple of days early to acclimate to the change.

Make sure you write down when and where you are to pick up your race packet. I once arrived at an out-of-town race five minutes before the race expo closed—and there wasn't packet pickup on race morning. Let's just say it made for a very stressful packet pickup and start to my race weekend. I also got stuck in traffic for hours the night before one race and missed packet pickup completely. Luckily, I had the phone number for the race and was able to call them and make arrangements to pick up my packet the morning of the race. If there is a race contact number, keep it with you as you travel. That can come in very handy for dealing with surprises.

Your training is over, so start packing now so you'll have time to shop for any last-minute needs. Here's a checklist you can use and add to as needed:

☑ running shoes (with timing chip attached - we will discuss this shortly)
☑ running shirt (with race bib attached - we will discuss this shortly)
☑ running bra (women)

- ☑ running shorts/pants
- ☑ undergarments
- ☑ running socks
- ☑ running hat/ear warmers, head bands
- ☑ hair elastics
- ☑ sunglasses
- ☑ stop watch
- ☑ race pace bracelet
- ☑ acetaminophen or ibuprofen for after the race
- ☑ throw-away clothes for the cold morning (gloves, hat, sweatshirt, pants, arm warmers)
- ☑ sandals for after the race
- ☑ change of clothes for after race (a must if you sweat a lot when you run)
- ☑ BodyGlide or Vaseline® for chafing
- ☑ race pouch, if you are going to carry one
- ☑ cash
- ☑ breakfast food, in case your hotel does not have appropriate breakfast choices
- ☑ adhesive bandages
- ☑ Biofreeze® or other numbing gel
- ☑ sunscreen
- ☑ extra safety pins
- ☑ permanent marker

This is also a good time to tell any family or friends who will be at the race how they can prepare. Here's a checklist for them:

- ☑ Make signs.
- ☑ Use noise makers.
- ☑ Cheer for everyone, not just the runners you know. You never know, your cheers might be the thing that encourages a weary runner to finish!

☑ Bring snacks and drinks because you might be there for a while, and post-race food is usually for runners only.

☑ Wear sunscreen/hats, comfy shoes, and layered clothes.

☑ Bring a camera to capture the race experience.

Two days before the race

This is a good time to review proper race etiquette. You'll be too preoccupied later in the week, so plant these things in your mind now and consider reviewing them in the car on the morning of the race:

- Look behind you before you change your direction.
- If you need to stop, such as to tie a shoe, look behind you and move to the side of the racecourse. Don't stop on the course.
- Walk through the water stops. It's much easier to drink while walking. I have choked, spilled sports drink down my front, and gotten some up my nose while trying to drink and run. The 10 seconds of walking will feel great; it's safer; and you will be able to drink more than if you speed through the drink station.
- If you need to spit, blow your nose, or spit out your drink, look around before you do it so nothing gross lands on runners near you.
- When throwing off any keep-warm clothes, make your way to the edge of the course and throw them off to the side.
- Say thank you to the volunteers, police, and medics who support the race.
- Stay alert!
- Encourage those around you—especially those who seem to be struggling.

The day before the race

Packet pickup

The organizers will have a packet for all runners to pick up before the race. Some smaller races allow you to pick up your race packet the morning of the race, but most require that you get it the day before. If you have the option to pick it up the morning of the event, prepare to get to the race very early to allow for long lines. There is nothing worse than spending the entire time before the race in the packet pickup line feeling rushed about getting your race number and timing chip.

If your event has a race expo at packet pickup, plan to spend an hour or two walking through the different expo booths. Race expos are great places to buy running gear, see the latest technology, sample different running fuels, and learn about other upcoming races. I love the atmosphere of race expos! There is electricity in the air as all the different runners come together to prepare for the race. If you decide to buy any running gear, though, remember that you shouldn't wear it on race day, no matter how tempting.

Equipment check

As soon as you get back from picking up your packet, lay out all of your race clothes from top to bottom to make sure you have everything. I once realized at 11 p.m. the night before a race that I had left my running bra at home. Not the best time to discover a key piece of clothing is missing! I had to take a midnight trip to a twenty-four hour discount store and buy every sports bra they had in my size, and then come back and spend more time trying to find the best fit. It was a stressful couple of hours, to say the least, and then I had to run in a new sports bra on race day—a *huge* no-no!—risking chafing and blisters.

This also prevents you from discovering the morning of the race that you left your running shoes in the car which is parked in the hotel garage seven floors down! Not that I've ever done that, of course…

If you're going to carry a pouch for things like your phone and gels, throw in an adhesive bandage or two, and a sample packet of Biofreeze or other numbing gel. That way, if you can't find a medical tent and you need a bandage for a blister or some numbing gel on an achy joint, you can stop for a few seconds right where you are.

There have been many races where numbing gel was a lifesaver for my knees. I will never forget one race running with a sore IT band[2], where I spent several miles looking for the next medic tent only to learn that the medic tents didn't have numbing gel! It was emotionally devastating because I had kept myself going with the thought that the gel would make the pain go away—and instead, I had to run through it. I now keep the little packets I receive at races in my pockets while I run. If nothing else, it helps me psychologically to know I have it if I need it.

Stand and be counted

Get the race bib out of your packet and write your emergency contact info on the back of your race number with a permanent marker. Of course, nothing bad is going to happen during the race, but this precaution only takes a moment. If your race number doesn't have a built-in timing device, wad it up and then flatten it back out before attaching it to your shirt. This makes it more flexible so the stiffness won't annoy you while you run. Pin your race number to the front of your race shirt—not on the back or on your shorts. I use four pins to attach my number because it's really annoying having it fly around while you run if you only attached it at the top. Once you have pinned it, try on your shirt. This is the time to discover and fix lopsided numbers!

Timing chips

If the timing device isn't built into your race number, check your packet for it. It will probably be a thin plastic disc that you attach to one of your shoes with a zip-tie passed under the laces. Check the packet for any directions regarding the timing. If there isn't one in your packet, your event may require you to pick it up race morning. Be sure you know when and where to pick it up. The packet should let you know if this is a one-time chip that you can throw away, or if a volunteer will snip the zip-tie from your shoelace after the race.

Many races are moving to the D-tag timing system, which is a sturdy piece of paper probably attached to your race number. You peel the D-tag from your number, slide one end underneath your shoelaces and back out, then stick the two ends together. Be careful not to flatten the D-tag, but leave it rounded over your laces (thus the "D" shape) with the race number on the top. D-tags are disposable, so you can just cut it from your shoe and throw it out after the race.

As I mentioned, still other races incorporate the timing device right into the race number. Some of my girlfriends experienced this new timing device in their latest half marathon and said it was their favorite timing device yet. And by the time this book is a year old, there will probably be a half dozen more new and improved timing devices! My point is to make sure you know what method your race is using, and that you know how to use it.

Taking care of your number and timing chip now will ensure you don't accidentally forget either of these critical pieces of equipment in the rush of the morning. There is nothing worse than discovering you left your timing chip back in the hotel or at home and your race won't be officially counted! Many bigger races won't let you in the start area without a race number, so forgetting it means you don't get to race at all!

Logistics

Plan your transportation to/from the race now. Will you be parking there? Do you need to have cash ready for the fee? How far away will you need to park? Sometimes the race start is a couple of miles from the parking area, so you will need to allow enough time for the walk to the start. Is there a runner drop-off area so you don't start your day with that long walk?

Traffic to the start can also be very heavy as 15,000 people try to get to race start at the same time. If there is transportation, figure out when you need to be ready to be picked up. Will your family and friends go to the race start with you or will they meet up with you later?

Post-race prep

Check the packet to see if your race has a bag check. Many races provide a place to leave personal items you don't want to carry while you run, such as a phone, money, keys, sandals, and a change of clothes. *TIP: Post-race sandals are a must!! Your feet will thank you if you have something like flip-flops to change into right after a race.* Checking a bag is a great option if you don't have friends or family coming along who can hold your belongings during the race. Be forewarned, though, that you usually have to check your bag as soon as you get to the starting area. That's why I suggested throwaway clothes—you won't be able to use bag check to stash the things you wear to keep warm while waiting for the race to start. The race packet should have specific instructions on how to label and check your bag.

Be sure there is some cash in your bag. Sometimes, after-party activities have a cost (such as massages and race souvenirs), and a lot of booths won't take credit cards.

Take some time to look in the race packet for the layout of the area around the finish line, and decide where you will meet friends and other runners after the race. It can be difficult to find people at the finish—especially if it is a big race. I once failed to arrange a meeting place with the friends I was running with because our plan was to run together the entire race. Instead, we got separated at the third mile and I never did find them. After searching for two hours at the finish, I finally gave up and went back to the hotel.

Even if your family watches you cross the finish line, they may still have a hard time getting to you after the race. It can take a while to maneuver through the crowds of finishers, get your medal, and wind through the finish area. Having a preset meeting place will help everyone find each other once you have crossed the finish line.

Many of the bigger races now have text message or Facebook notifications so that for a nominal fee your family can receive alerts when you cross certain mileage points. This is a great way for people to keep track of your race. If they are attempting to see you at points along the way, this will help them decide where they will catch up with you on the course.

Body preparation
Steer clear of high-fiber foods and dairy products today, if they tend to upset your stomach when you run. I usually stick with easily digestible foods the day before a race—foods I have practiced with and know do not upset my stomach. Sip on water and/or sports drink all day. Your urine should be pale yellow and plentiful. Just drinking a huge glass before bed will not hydrate you! Eat an early dinner, and no more than usual. Tonight is not the night to eat a double portion of pasta and chicken. Eating a bigger than normal portion can lead to an upset stomach. Don't worry—if you have eaten well during the week, your glycogen stores should be loaded up and ready to go! And avoid spicy foods, gassy foods, and anything you've never eaten before. Some suggestions:

- bland pasta with lean beef or chicken
- chicken and rice
- plain fish and rice or pasta
- turkey sandwich

While we're talking about the needs of our bodies, this is a good time to examine the race map in your packet and locate the aid stations along the course. Decide now which ones will be your cue to take the carb fuel you've chosen. Practice your mental exercises, go to bed early, and set two alarms—just in case one doesn't go off.

The morning of the race

☑ Get up early enough to do everything you need to do without feeling rushed. Eat a good breakfast of the things you've practiced eating before your long runs. Take your time in the bathroom.

☑ Spend some time in prayer, thanking God for helping you through all this training and for giving you the strength to do this. Ask for His help—both physical and mental—through the day. Ask Him to help you be an encouragement to other runners.

☑ This is my last reminder—*do not try **anything** new on race day*. No new food, no new gels, no new clothes, no new shoes, no new deodorant... NOTHING NEW!

☑ You need to be sipping on water all morning, and take a bottle with you to the start area. When you get there after you've picked up your packet and/or checked a bag as necessary, immediately get in line for a port-a-potty. Everyone else has been sipping water all morning and the lines get very long. You definitely want to be able to go to the bathroom before the race starts!

Remind yourself to *have fun!* Enjoy the experience. Don't worry about things you can't control.

Final thoughts

I know this has been a lot of information, but most of it is really common sense, and not all of it applies to every race. Just highlight those points that apply to you and don't worry about the rest. Remember not to panic if something goes wrong. I've tried to give you an exhaustive preparation list, but even if you forget a key article of clothing or you get to the race starting area late, don't let it get to you—you will still have a great race! I have done so many things wrong (how else would I know so many things to put in this chapter?) and have still had great races.

You can practice and prepare for the rest of your life or you can just get out and do it, knowing you have done everything you can to get ready. Sometimes you just have to jump into the race. Run your race. Enjoy the journey. Take the time to breathe in the sights and sounds of the race. Lift up those around you, and shine His light through your race. Determine now that when you start mile 11, moving into mileage you may have never before run, you *will* put one foot in front of the other until you see the finish line. Don't quit! This is what you have prepared for, and now it's time to celebrate all that effort!

Why bother?

Personally, the reason I choose to train, day after day, year after year, and the reason I enter and run races, is because with each training program and each race I get just the tiniest hint of what it will be like when I cross the most important finish line in my life. I will never forget the day, while running a long training run for my 50K, that it hit me why I run. Life was busy. Work was tough. I felt like God wasn't hearing my prayers. The 50K training program was much harder than I'd expected. I had been sick and had missed almost two weeks of training and felt like I would never catch back up. I felt guilty for the time I spent running and not with my family. It just didn't seem worth it, and as I ran that day, I was seriously contemplating quitting. In fact, I had already told one of my children I was pretty

Is there a time to give yourself permission to drop out of a race? Yes…if you feel dizzy, have severe diarrhea or vomiting, or stop sweating. There are times your physical health outweighs finishing a race. Be smart. Remember, there is always another race, and your health is more important than a medal.

sure I wasn't going to run the race. I was in my own little world, feeling pretty sorry for myself, not paying attention to the music playing over my earbuds. The blazing sun was sucking out what little energy I had left. I was tired and was about to just stop running when I became aware of the words being poured into my head: *You and I run for the prize that lies ahead... Get up, this race can be won.*[3]

It was as if God was speaking to me, telling me not to give up, that there was a purpose for my running, if I just kept putting one foot in front of the other. As these words pierced my soul, an image of me running the race of my life filled my head. Along the racecourse were friends and family—people I loved and who loved me, cheering for me and telling me to keep running, I was almost there. Up ahead was the finish line, a huge ribbon waiting for me to run through and break. Not only was I finishing this race, I was going to win! As I ran strong to the finish, I saw that it was Jesus holding the ribbon. Just for me. I ran through the ribbon and into His arms. The only race that really matters, I won.

I will never win a physical race on this earth, but every race I finish gets me closer to the one and only race I will win—if I just don't quit. That's why I run. And it was after finishing my 50K, relying on God to get me through and giving Him the glory for being able to finish, that I realized He wanted me to share my journey with others.

Look, you may not relate to why I love to run and how I find God in the midst of my runs. That's okay; but seek Him, and find Him. He desperately wants to reveal Himself to you. It may not be through running for you, but I feel connected to my Creator through my runs so naturally I desire that connection for you—in whatever you pursue. You have a race to run, a plan to follow, and a purpose to fulfill. Seek Him in all you do and He will reveal your race to you.

I am so excited for you to run your race!

Week 13

The Finish Line;
What's Next?

On the seventh day God had finished his work of creation,
so he rested from all his work.
Genesis 2:2

Congratulations! You did it! You trained, you raced, and you finished. I hope your legs have had a few days to recover and are beginning to feel less sore. I am almost always sore for a few days after I run a half marathon. After a really fast race, I may be very sore for several days, and even have a hard time walking up and down stairs! A couple of times a day, spend 10 to 20 minutes icing any areas that are especially sore such as quads, knees, and hamstrings. The ice will decrease inflammation and aid in recovery.

This week, pamper yourself a little—you deserve it! Get some extra sleep and—if possible—a sports massage. Tell the massage therapist to concentrate on your sore legs. It'll hurt, but you will feel so much better afterwards. Continue to eat healthy carbs (whole grains, fruits, and veggies) and drink fluids. You need to replenish the glycogen stores in your muscles and any lost fluids. Remember, carbohydrates are stored in water, so your weight may be a bit higher than normal as your body recovers.

If you look at the next two weeks of training (see Appendix E for Weeks 13 and 14), you will notice we are still running. A good rule of thumb for recovery after a race is one day of recovery for each mile raced. For a half marathon, that means thirteen days of recovery. However, recovery does not mean no running. Recovery means easy, slow runs. Your body will actually feel better if you run a little over the next couple of weeks. If you feel your muscles are too sore to run, even a slow, easy walk will loosen up stiff muscles and speed up recovery.

This week, let's look back on our race while it's still fresh in our memories. Now is the time to see what went well, what didn't go so well, and set our sights on new goals. What was the single best thing about the race itself (the crowds, the finish line party, the medal…)?

_____

_____

What was the single worst thing about the race (not enough water stations, too many people)?

_____

_____

If you could have changed one thing about the race, what would it have been?

_____

_____

What aspect of the race would you love to do again?

_____

_____

Some people discover that they dislike big, crowded races. They don't enjoy having to stand at the start so long, and weaving in and out of the crowds of runners during the race. Others find they dislike smaller races, with minimal spectator and crowd support. I personally find I like big races when I am running just for fun or with a group of new runners, and smaller races when I want to run fast. I pick my races based on what experience I want to have.

Now that we have reflected on the race experience itself, let's take some time to think about your personal experience within that race. What did you discover about yourself during the race?

_____

_____

What did you discover about God during the race?

_____

_____

Did you meet your pace goals? If you did, think about what helped you reach your goal. If you didn't, why do you think you missed your goal?

_____

_____

Did you meet your performance goal(s)? Explain why or why not:

_____

_____

Perhaps, for whatever reason, you were not able to finish your race. I know how frustrating and depressing that can be, but don't be discouraged—sometimes it's just not our race. Whether you didn't even start the race or you had to stop before you reached the finish line, look at this experience as a learning process, not a failure. Even elite runners have races they don't finish. Instead, look back and try to determine what you need to tweak in order to have a successful race next time around.

Why do you think you were not able to finish your race? What can you do differently next time?

_____

_____

_____

_____

Unless injury is preventing you from running or your better judgment says to hold off, I encourage you to look ahead a few weeks and find a race to run. Go back to Week 5 of our training, and keep moving forward. Some people have to work harder than others to get to that start line. I'm not a natural runner. I have to work hard to get to my race starts, but the reward is so very worth it. Don't give up!

Over the next couple of weeks as you recover, you may find yourself with a mix of emotions, ranging from:

- feeling a little depressed, or
- never wanting to run again, to
- feeling ready to run a race again as soon as possible.

Circle the feeling above that most closely resembles how you are feeling this week.

If you're feeling blue, you're not alone. Many runners feel let down after a race. After all, you just spent 12 weeks of your life training, leading up to an emotionally and physically exhausting day of racing, and now it's all over! Some runners are especially depressed if they didn't make one or more of their goals. Allow yourself to be sad for a couple for days, but don't stay there. Go back over your training plan. See how far you have come, what you may need to tweak for next time, and then focus on the next challenge.

If you finished your race and said, "I never want to do that again," you are also not alone! In fact, I have uttered those words many times! I told myself I would never run a particular race again (and have since run it two more times—but with different goals), and I told myself I would never run another mountain ultra-marathon after I finished my 50K. Three years later, I'm running a 50-mile race. Give yourself some time and you will probably decide it was a good experience, and you are ready to challenge yourself again!

If you finished your race and are raring to go again, great...but if this is your first race, I highly suggest you take some time to recover before jumping into another half marathon race—especially if you ran really hard. Your body needs time to rest and recoup. Yes, some people can run race after race, weekend after weekend. Keep in mind, they are probably not *racing* these races, but are running them at a very easy pace—and have spent a long time building up a strong foundation. For those of you new to racing, I suggest taking six weeks before you race again: two weeks to recover, three weeks to build back up, and one week to taper before you race again. If you insist on racing before then, then just run at an easy pace rather than at race pace.

If after two weeks of recovery you are feeling ready to go, a great compromise is to enter a local 5K or 10K. It won't be as hard on your body and you can still be a part of the exciting race atmosphere.

Looking to the future

When you have recovered, I encourage you to set new goals. Keep running! Don't let this be your one and only race. I enter race after race after race (but I allow recovery in between!) because they motivate me to keep moving, to keep growing. God teaches me something new in each race I run.

I encourage you to hang your race medal proudly to remind you of your accomplishment. I have hooks in my office where I hang my race medals. They are a constant reminder of how far I have come, how hard I have worked, and how awesome God is. Keep your race number as a souvenir. I have one friend who writes the race info and her race time on the back of each of her race numbers and keeps them in an album. Buy a 13.1 sticker for your car window or bumper. Be proud of being a runner! Whether you realize it or not, you are inspiring others to begin their own running program because they have watched you train and then successfully complete a race. You are inspiring someone else to run his or her own race.

One of the ladies from my very first marathon training group, through her diligent training and positive attitude, has inspired her husband, sons, sisters, brothers-in-law, aunt, and friends to train for and run half marathons and marathons. For years, her family watched her train, struggle, persevere, and finish. One by one they began joining her in her races. Now they are all training and running together.

When I think about it, that's what I strive for in my own Christian walk; that through my actions, attitude, and ability to persevere and keep my eyes on the prize, that I draw people to Him; to be a light that shines a beacon of hope. As Jesus Himself said in Matthew 5:16, "Let your light shine before others, that they may see your good deeds and glorify your Father in heaven" (TNIV).

As we wrap up this training program, I have one last thought for you to ponder. When you reached your finish line, did you feel like you left everything on the racecourse or did you get to the finish line and realize you could have given it more effort?

_____

_____

The races I'm most proud of and have the fondest memories of, regardless of my finish time and whether or not I accomplished the goals I set, are those races where I gave it everything I had. I left it all on the course. When I crossed the finish line, I knew there wasn't another ounce of energy left in my body. For me, those races are the physical manifestation of my desire to give everything I have to my Lord and Savior—to reach my finish line, knowing I gave it everything I had, that I left nothing behind.

That is my prayer for you and your life—to persevere; to be a beacon of light to those around you struggling in their own races; to keep putting one foot in front of the other, and to give it all to Him who loves you more than you can ever fathom. I pray Hebrews 12:1 that you, with perseverance, continue to run the race that God has set before you, physically and spiritually. I am so very proud of you and can't wait to meet you at the finish line!

Physical Activity Readiness Questionnaire

If you are planning to become much more physically active than you are now, start by answering the seven questions in the box below. If you are between the ages of 15 and 69, the PAR-Q will tell you if you should check with your doctor before you start. If you are over 69 years of age, and you are not used to being very active, check with your doctor.

Common sense is your best guide when you answer these questions. Please read the questions carefully and answer each one honestly: check YES or NO, and then read the next page.

YES	NO	
		Has your doctor ever said that you have a heart condition and that you should only do physical activity recommended by a doctor?
		Do you feel pain in your chest when you do physical activity?
		In the past month, have you had chest pain when you were not doing physical activity?
		Do you lose your balance because of dizziness or do you ever lose consciousness?
		Do you have a bone or joint problem (for example, back, knee or hip) that could be made worse by a change in your physical activity?
		Is your doctor currently prescribing drugs (for example, water pills) for your blood pressure or heart condition?
		Do you know of any other reason why you should not do physical activity?

If you answered *YES* to one or more questions:

- Talk with your doctor by phone or in person BEFORE you start becoming much more physically active. Tell your doctor about the PAR-Q and which questions you answered YES.
- You may be able to do any activity you want—as long as you start slowly and build up gradually. Or, you may need to restrict your activities to those which are safe for you. Talk with your doctor about the kinds of activities you wish to participate in (particularly preparing for a half marathon) and follow his or her advice.

If you answered *NO* to all questions:

If you answered NO honestly to all PAR-Q questions, you can be reasonably sure that you can start becoming much more physically active. Begin slowly and build up gradually. But note:

Delay becoming much more active:
• if you are not feeling well because of a temporary illness such as a cold or a fever–wait until you feel better.
• if you are or may be pregnant–talk to your doctor before you start becoming more active.

If your health changes so that you then answer YES to any of the above questions, tell your fitness or health professional. Ask whether you should change your physical activity plan.

The PAR-Q form was designed by the Canadian Society for Exercise Physiology. Used with permission.

Warm-Up and Stretching

If you read ten different running articles you will probably get ten different opinions on stretching. Some say never stretch before you run, some say only do dynamic (moving) stretches. Some say stretch after you have run 5-10 minutes, others say stretch only after you run!

I believe a few minutes of easy, dynamic stretches before—or in the first 5-10 minutes of—walking are fine. I also find that I feel much better if I take a few minutes to lightly stretch my muscles after I finish. However, stretching is as individual as running so listen to your body! The stretches below will help you stretch from head to toe. Use them as a guideline to discover the stretching routine that works best for you.

Warm up stretches

Dynamic stretching, consisting of controlled movements that improve your range of motion, does more than just help loosen up muscles. It also increases your heart rate, body temperature, and blood flow. The dynamic stretches listed below target the muscles you will use for running. Start with small, slow movements. As your muscles warm up you can increase the range of motion. *Never* force a stretch. If any stretch causes pain, *stop immediately.*

- **Shoulder shrugs:** shrug your shoulders up and down, then front to back. Repeat 5 times.

- **Hip openers:** stand with your feet hip-width apart, toes facing forward. Bring your right knee up so your thigh is parallel to the ground. Keep that leg angle at 90 degrees throughout the exercise. Slowly open the right hip, rotating your knee to outside. Make sure the ankle and knee stay in line as your hip rotates. Repeat this 5 times, then switch sides and do the same with the left leg. You can use a wall for balance, if needed.

- **Forward leg swings:** stand with your feet hip-width apart, toes facing forward. Keeping your right leg straight but relaxed, swing the entire right leg forward from the hip. Relax, and allow gravity to swing the leg back behind your body. (Allow your knee and ankle to follow the hip rotation as it goes behind your body. Your hip, knee and ankle should stay aligned.) This is a slow, gentle movement, so don't overswing the leg. Repeat 10 times, then switch to the left leg. You can use a wall for balance, if necessary.

- **Side leg swings:** stand with your feet hip-width apart, toes facing forward. Keeping your right leg straight but relaxed, swing the entire right leg out to the side. Then relax and allow gravity to swing it back, crossing in front of your body to the left side. Again, this should be a slow, gentle movement, so don't overswing the leg. Repeat 10 times, then switch to the left leg. You can use a wall for balance, but it may restrict your motion.

- **Walking lunges:** stand with your feet hip-width apart, toes facing forward. Step forward with your right leg, using a large stride. Make sure to keep your right knee over—or just behind—your toes. Drop your left knee toward the ground. Maintain a tight core and upright posture. Now bring your left leg forward and repeat the motion starting with a left leg stride. Repeat each side 10 times.

- **Straight leg walk:** lace your fingers together, and lift both arms straight out in front of your body. Keeping your back and knees straight, walk forward, lifting your legs straight out and flexing your toes. Try to touch your toes to your hands with each step. (You can lower your arms if needed to help them touch your legs.)

- **Grapevine:** alternate crossing your right foot in front of, and behind, your left leg as you move sideways along the ground. Allow your hips, core, and chest to twist with the movement. Repeat 10 times and then switch directions and legs.

- **Skips:** skip forward, taking nice big steps. Then skip sideways in each direction. Repeat this for about 30 seconds.

- **Ankle rolls:** Standing on your left leg, roll your right ankle to the outside for a count of 10, then inside for a count of ten. Now repeat this with your left ankle.

Cool down stretches

Static stretching, consisting of gently holding a stretch for at least 30 seconds, is designed to gently elongate your tired, tight muscles. You should not bounce or move as you gently stretch your muscles. The muscles should feel a gentle pull. If a stretch causes pain, *stop*. Doing these stretches on a regular basis will help increase your flexibility and range of motion. If you run out of time after your run, you can do these while watching TV or before bed.

- **Head rolls:** tilt your head to the left, gently pressing your ear toward your left shoulder. Now roll your head forward gently to the front and then right until your right ear is pressing toward your shoulder. Repeat 3 times.

- **Arm/shoulder stretch #1:** grab your upper right arm with your left hand. Using the left hand, gently pull the right arm in front of your body, parallel with the shoulder. Hold for a count of 10, and repeat on left side.

- **Arm/shoulder stretch #2:** lift your right arm straight up toward the ceiling, keeping the arm close to your right ear. Now bend your right arm at the elbow and allow your hand to fall behind your head. Use your left hand to grab your right arm just above the elbow and gently pull the right arm behind your head. Hold for a count of 10 and repeat on the left side.

- **Chest stretch:** clasp your hands together behind your back, interlocking your fingers. Now straighten both elbows and try to keep your hands close to your back. Hold for 10 seconds, then relax and repeat for another 10 seconds.

- **Standing hip flexor (psoas) stretch:** stand with your feet hip-width apart, toes facing forward. Take a large step forward with your right leg, bending the right knee. Keep your left leg straight, but relaxed (don't lock your left knee) and allow the left leg to slightly roll inwards, toward your body. Now scoop your pelvis forward, tucking your bottom underneath your hips. You should feel a stretch in the front of pelvis of the forward leg. Hold that position for 30 seconds. For an added stretch, you can lift your left arm up and over to the right side. Now switch sides and repeat.

- **Kneeling hip flexor stretch:** start in a half-kneeling position, with your right foot flat on floor, and your left knee on the ground directly under your hips. Make sure your back is straight and your hips, knees, and shoulders are aligned. Now tilt your pelvis forward, scooping your bottom underneath your hips. For added stretch you can lean slightly forward, but don't lose the pelvis tilt as you do this. Hold for 30 seconds, and switch sides.

- **Inner thigh (adductor) stretch:** stand with your feet straddled wide, with your right foot slightly forward. The big toe of your left foot should be even with the arch of your right foot. Now slowly shift your weight to the right in a lunge, allowing the right knee to bend. Hold for 30 seconds, then switch sides—making sure to realign your feet.

- **Standing quad stretch:** stand with your feet hip-width apart, toes facing forward. Bending your right leg at the knee, lift your foot behind you, grabbing your ankle from behind with the left hand. Be sure to keep your right knee directly underneath the hip. Now pull your right ankle back and tighten your glutes until the stretch is felt in your upper thigh. *Stop if you feel pain in your back.* Hold for 30 seconds, then switch sides.

- **Lying quad stretch:** lie on your stomach. Bend your knees and grab both ankles with your hands. Tighten your glutes to feel a stretch in both quads. For more of a stretch, you can lift your knees off the ground. Hold for 30 seconds.

- **Standing iliotibial band stretch:** holding onto a wall for balance, lift your right ankle onto your left thigh. Now bend your left leg as though you were going to sit in a chair. You should feel the stretch in both glute and hip. Hold for 30 seconds, then switch legs.

- **Sitting iliotibial band stretch:** sit on the ground with your right leg out straight and your left leg out to side. Now move your feet toward you, bend both knees to 90 degree angles. Lean over the right leg to feel a stretch in your glute and hip. Hold for 30 seconds, then switch legs.

- **Hamstring stretch #1:** stand with your right foot back and left foot forward, with your legs straight. Now bend your left leg and bend at the hips as though you were going to sit. Lean over your straight right leg to feel a stretch in hamstring. Hold for 30 seconds, then switch legs.

- **Hamstring stretch #2:** stand with your feet hip-width apart, toes facing forward. Lift your right leg, placing it on a step or chair at about hip height. Now lean slowly forward, keeping your back straight until you feel stretch in the back of your thigh. Hold for 30 seconds, then switch legs.

- **Lower calf stretch:** stand in front of a wall with your right foot back and both knees bent. Keeping your right heel on the floor, turned slightly out, lean into the wall until a stretch is felt in your lower calf. Hold for 30 seconds, then switch legs.

- **Upper calf stretch:** stand in front of a wall with your right foot back, leg straight, and your left leg bent. Keeping your right heel on the floor, lean into the wall until a stretch is felt in your upper calf. Hold for 30 seconds, then switch legs.

- **Ankle rolls:** slowly roll each ankle to the outside 10 times, then to the inside 10 times.

- **Plantar Fascia (arch of foot) stretch:** Stand with only the ball of your right foot on the edge of a stair or curb. Push your heel down until a stretch is felt through your arch. Hold for 30 seconds, then switch feet.

- **Squat stretch:** This is great for after a long run! With your feet wider than your shoulders and toes slightly turned out, slowly squat down. Make sure your toes and knees stay in line. Keep your head up, above your heart. Rest there a minute, breathing deeply. Stand up slowly, using a wall or friend for support if you feel wobbly.

Appendix C

Core Exercises

There are many excellent core and strength training exercises to choose from. I have picked a few basic ones that are extremely effective at strengthening your core. Along with the basic exercises I have included some *regressions* to make them a bit easier and *progressions* to make them more challenging.

I also have a couple of pieces of equipment that I use on a regular basis:
- stability ball—there are different sizes, so choose the one that is made for your height. It will give the height range on the packaging.
- light dumbbell weights—I have 5 lb. weights that I use a lot.

Don't feel like you have to have these pieces of equipment. You can strengthen your entire body without equipment, using just your body weight.

1) Standard plank: lie face down on the floor. Engage your core by pulling your belly button into your spine. Place your hands beside your shoulders and push your body up onto your hands and the tips of your toes, which are about shoulder width apart. Your hands and toes should be the only thing touching the floor. Like a push-up, you should keep your bottom tight and your body in a straight line from your ankles to your shoulders. Do not allow your back to arch or your bottom to sag. Your shoulders should be directly above your wrists. Your neck should be relaxed and your head in line with your body so that your eyes are gazing at the floor in front of you. Hold for 5-10 seconds, trying to work up to 30 seconds.

Regression: push up to your forearms instead of your hands. Make sure your elbows are directly under your shoulders.

Further regression: push your body up to your knees instead of your toes. This one can be done using your forearms, then progressing to your hands.

Progression: after pushing up into plank position, slowly lift your right foot off the ground a few inches, making sure your body stays tight and level. Slowly lower your foot back to the ground and then lift your left foot. Repeat 5 times each side.

More progression: kneeling on the ground, rest your forearms on the stability ball. Push up into a plank position and hold, maintaining your balance on the ball. For added strength, use your elbows to slowly roll the ball out in front of you. (This is a very small movement!)

Another option: place your feet on the stability ball, with your hands and knees on the floor. Push up into a plank position, make sure your hands stay directly below your shoulders. Maintain proper plank form while staying balanced on the stability ball.

Further progression: push up to a forearm plank position, with your weight on your forearms and toes. From there, pushing with right arm first, then left, push up to standard plank position. Hold for a few seconds and lower back down to a forearm plank, starting with right arm. Start with right side 5 times, then switch to left side for five. Make sure you keep your core tight throughout and as you raise and lower your arms try not to twist your body!

2) Standard Side Plank: lie on your right side, with your left foot on top of your right foot. Lift your upper body, supporting it with your right forearm.

Engage your core by pushing your belly button into your spine. Now lift your hips off the floor, moving your left hip toward the ceiling, so your body is supported by your right forearm and right foot. Your left arm can help support your body by resting on the floor in front of you or (better) can be raised up to the ceiling. Don't let your hips sag or roll forward—you want them to stay in line with the rest of your body. Hold for 10 seconds (building up to 30), and lower your hips back to the floor. Then switch to the left side and repeat.

Regression: allow your left foot to rest on the floor in front of your right foot.

Further regression: raise your hips up but keep your knees and lower legs on the ground.

Progression: instead of your forearm, raise up to your hand—making sure your wrist is directly below your shoulder.

Further progression: as you hold your side plank, your upper arm extended toward the ceiling, slowly reach your upper arm forward and cross it under your body. Keep your hips in line, so you're twisting from the core. To make it more challenging, hold a small weight in your upper arm as you twist. Repeat 10-15 times, then switch sides.

Another progression: from a forearm side plank, allow your bottom hip to dip to the floor, then pull it back up into the plank position. Don't allow your hips to sag. Repeat 10-15 times, then switch sides.

3) **Standard push up:** push ups are a terrific way to strengthen your entire body! Begin by raising into a standard plank. Then slowly bend your arms, lowering your body to the floor, getting as close to the floor with your nose as possible before raising back up to a plank. Make sure your wrists are directly

below your shoulders, and your core is engaged and level throughout the entire movement. Don't allow your bottom to sag or your back to arch. If this puts too much pressure on your wrists, *don't move them forward.* Instead, roll up a towel and place it under your palms to reduce the angle of your wrists.

Regression: push your body up to your knees instead of your toes, allowing your feet to lift off the ground as you raise and lower the upper part of your body. Keep your core tight, and don't allow your bottom to sag or your back to arch. Repeat 5-10 times. Once you have mastered this exercise, try to add one standard push up each workout.

Progression: stagger your hands so that the right is slightly above your shoulders and the left is slightly below them. Switch your hands every 5 push ups.

Another progression: raise one leg as you lower your body to the ground. Switch legs every 5 push ups.

Another progression: rest your feet on a stability ball. Raise and lower your body while maintaining balance on the ball.

4) **Inch worm:** from a standing position, engage your core and slowly roll down your spine until your hands are touching the floor in front of your feet. Walk your hands out away from your feet until you are in a standard plank position (your bottom will be in the air as you begin this—think inchworm movement). Hold for a few seconds, then slowly walk your feet up to your hands. Keep your core tight with as little side to side movement as possible.

Progression: add a push up each time you are in the plank position.

5) **Superman:** lie face down on the floor, with your arms resting above your

head. Engage your core and tighten your glutes. Simultaneously lift your head, raise your right arm, and lift your left foot several inches off the floor. A slow, small movement is all you need. If this puts too much pressure on your back, do not lift your arm and leg as high. Lower your head, arm and leg back to the floor. Now switch sides and repeat, continuing 10-15 times.

6) **Bridge:** lie on your back, with your knees bent 90 degrees and your feet flat on the floor. Engage your core and slowly lift your hips and your back off of the floor until your body forms a straight line from your shoulders to your knees. Squeeze your glutes at the top of the movement and don't let your bottom sag. Hold for 5-10 seconds, then lower back to the ground. Repeat 5-10 times.

Progression: straighten one leg once your hips are raised. Switch legs each time.

Another progression: rest your feet on a stability ball instead of the floor. Maintain your balance on the ball as you lift your hips and back.

Further progression: rest your feet on a stability ball instead of the floor. Once your hips are raised, lift one foot off of the ball—maintaining balance on the ball with your other foot.

Appendix D

Common Injuries, Warning Signs, & Treatments

These are a few common running injuries that most runners experience at one time or another, along with suggestions that may heal the injury. This is not an exhaustive list—just a few of the more common injuries, many of which I have experienced personally. My suggestions come from my own healing process as well as a variety of books I have read. *This information is in no way intended to take the place of your doctor's advice. Always seek proper medical attention if your pain is beyond normal muscle soreness, gets worse, and doesn't seem to get better with rest.*

Most of the time, running injuries occur because of:
- training errors. In other words, too much, too soon, too fast (adding too much mileage, too much speed, too many hills...)
- inadequate shoes. Either you are wearing the wrong shoes for your feet, or your shoes need to be replaced
- tight muscles surrounding the injured area.

You know you should stop running for a while when:
- the pain makes you alter your running gait.
- the pain lasts more than a couple of days and gets worse.
- you feel you have to take pain medication in order to get through your training.

Note: Never take NSAID-containing products (e.g. aspirin, ibuprofen, naproxene) before a run. Studies show that these products elevate your blood pressure, inhibit hormones that help normalize the blood flow to your kidneys, and block enzymes that protect your heart. Combine that with the exertion of running and slight dehydration and you have the possibility of serious, life threatening side effects. If you must take a pain reliever before you run, stick with products that contain acetaminophen. You can use NSAID products once you have finished your run and your body has recovered.

General injury treatment

Remember to RICE your injury:
Rest: take a day or two off from running. It is better to rest a couple of days than to aggravate your injury and end up having it sideline you for weeks.
Ice: use ice on the area for ten to twenty minutes, several times a day. Frozen water bottles are great for icing iliotibial bands and the arches of your feet, and frozen bags of veggies are great for icing knees.
Compression: an elastic bandage or other form of compression can help with swelling and inflammation. I love to wear compression socks and sleeves (sold at many specialty running stores) to help my muscles recover more quickly.
Elevation: elevating the injured area will also help reduce swelling.

Do-it-yourself massage:
A foam roller is an invaluable tool for sore muscles! It's a firm foam log 6 inches in diameter, available at most specialty running stores and big-box sporting goods stores. Using your body weight, *very slowly* roll your muscles (quads, calves, hamstrings, iliotibial bands, back) up and down the foam roller. When you come to a particularly painful spot, stay on that spot until you feel it release. Rolling your muscles on a foam roller breaks up knots that stretching alone can't release. Think of it as your very own personal massage therapist.

Specific injuries

My foot falls asleep when I run, or I have pain and pressure on the top of my foot when I run.
Although nerve issues can cause your feet to fall asleep or feel pain and pressure, most likely it is caused by the way your shoes are laced. There are dozens of different ways to lace and tie your running shoes. A good shoe specialist at your local running store should be able to help you determine the best lacing technique for your foot issue.

My toes tingle and burn. I feel like I have a lump under my toes when I run.
Morton's Neuroma is caused by pressure on the nerves around your toes. Many times it is due to wearing shoes that are too short or have a toe box that is too narrow. Possible treatments:
- wear correct fitting shoes
- adjust training schedule—cut down mileage
- use foot pads/supports to reduce pressure to forefoot
- ice and massage the area that hurts

The arch of my foot or my heel hurts, especially when I step out of bed first thing in the morning. It almost feels like I have a bruise on my heel.
Plantar Fasciitis is a common cause of heel and arch pain, occurring when the plantar fascia, the band that runs along the arch of your foot and connects at your heel bone and your toes, becomes irritated and inflamed. Tight calf muscles can cause the plantar facia to become irritated. Possible treatments:
- ice your arch several times a day (a frozen water bottle works well).
- stretch and foam roll your calf muscles.

- make sure your shoes aren't excessively worn and you are wearing the right shoe for your foot. You may need a shoe with more medial support and extra arch support.
- adjust your training schedule—cut down your mileage/speed.
- massage your calves and arch of your foot
- purchase night splints (these do not cure the problem, only reduce the pain upon waking)
- lose weight (extra body weight can stress the plantar fascia)
- physical therapy

My shins ache when I start running. The pain usually subsides after a few minutes, but returns after I finish running. My entire shinbone is tender and sore.

"Shin Splints" is the general term used for pain along the shinbone. Usually the pain is caused by inflammation where the muscles attach to the shinbone. A common cause of shin splints is tight calf muscles. Possible treatments:

- ice your shinbones several times a day
- stretch and foam roll your calf muscles
- adjust your training schedule—cut down your mileage/speed
- reduce hill work, which can aggravate shin splints
- make sure your shoes aren't excessively worn and you are wearing the right shoe for your foot. You may need a shoe with more medial support and extra arch support.
- physical therapy

Note: There are other injuries that can cause pain similar to shin splints, such as stress fractures and compartment syndrome. A stress fracture is a small crack in the bone, and is typically a more localized pain rather than an all-over shin pain. Compartment syndrome is a serious condition where pressure builds up within the muscle compartments of the lower legs. It is usually accompanied by cramping, burning, and swelling to the muscle while running, which stops at rest. It is wise to visit a medical professional to determine the exact cause of pain.

The outside of my knee hurts (a lot!) when I start running, but there is no swelling. Sometimes the pain is so bad I have to stop running, and it seems to be getting worse. It also hurts when I walk down stairs.
Iliotibial Band Syndrome is caused when your iliotibial band (ITB), which is a long band of fascia that runs from your outer hip to below your knee, becomes irritated. Left untreated, it will get worse until the pain is present with almost all activity. Usually ITB Syndrome is caused by excessive internal rotation of the leg caused by pronation (toes pointed out or in rather than straight), poor running biomechanics, and poor flexibility and strength. Rarely, it can be caused by running on a slanted surface (such as the shoulder of a road).
Possible treatments:

- ice the outside of your thigh
- foam roll and stretch your quads, ITB, and glutes
- strengthen your glutes
- rest!
- make sure your shoes aren't excessively worn and you are wearing the right shoe for your foot. You may need a shoe with more medial support and extra arch support.
- physical therapy
- massage your ITB
- run on flat, not slanted, surfaces

The area under and around my kneecap hurts when I run.
"Runner's Knee" is the all-encompassing name given to the variety of aches and pains runners experience in and around their knees. The most common is Patello Femoral Pain Syndrome (PFPS). You may have heard the myth that runners experience more knee arthritis and degeneration than non-runners, however recent studies are finding that running does not necessarily cause otherwise healthy knees to breakdown. Usually, knee pain is caused by improper tracking of the knee due to muscle imbalance. Possible treatments:

- rest
- ice the knee
- foam roll and stretch the calves, quads, and hamstrings
- strengthen the quads, glutes, hamstrings
- wear a knee brace for additional support
- make sure your shoes aren't excessively worn and you are wearing the right shoe for your foot. You may need a shoe with more medial support and extra arch support.
- physical therapy

My outer buttocks muscle is tender and I sometimes have pain radiating down the back of the same leg.
Piriformis Syndrome is caused by a tight piriformis, a small muscle deep in your buttocks. Sometimes a tight piriformis can put pressure on the sciatic nerve, which runs very close to the muscle—in some people the nerve actually runs through the muscle fiber—causing pain to radiate down your leg. Proper stretching and warming up go a long way toward relieving piriformis syndrome. Possible treatments:

- rest
- ice the area that hurts
- stretch the adductor (inner thigh) muscles

- use a tennis ball to massage the tender area (stand against a wall or sit on the ball and use your body weight to massage the muscle)
- strengthen your hips, lower back, abductor (outer thigh) and buttocks muscles
- physical therapy

Again, these suggestions are not meant to take the place of a visit to your doctor or physical therapist. There are many terrific sports injury books available as well. One book I have found to be particularly helpful is Janet Hamilton's *Running Strong & Injury Free.*

Appendix E — Full Workout Schedule

ER = Easy Run, X-train = Cross Train, LR = Long Run

Week	Workout 1	Workout 2	Workout 3	Workout 4	Workout 5	Workout 6	Workout 7
1	ER 35 min	X-train 30 min	ER 30 min	ER 35 min	Rest	LR 5 miles	Rest
2	ER 35 min	X-train 30 min	ER 30 min	ER 40 min	Rest	LR 6 miles	Rest
3	ER 40 min	X-train 30 min + 20 min core	ER 35 min	ER 45 min + 10 min core	Rest	LR 7 miles	Rest
4	ERun 35 min	X-train 30 min + 20 min core	ER 35 min	ER 40 min + 10 min core	Rest	LR 5 miles	Rest
5	ER 40-50 min	X-train 30 min + 20 min core	ER 35 min (spend 10 on form)	5 min of form exercises. + ER 45 min + 10 min core	Rest	LR 8 miles (concentrate on form for 2)	Rest
6	ER 40-50 min (spend 10 on form)	X-train 30 min + 20 min core	ER 35 min OR Easy 10 + Hard 15 + Easy 10	ER 45 min + 10 min core	Find delta heart rate	LR 9 miles (in mile 8 do 5 strides, 30 sec. each)	Rest
7	ER 50-60 min OR Easy 10 + Race 20 + Easy 30	X-train 30 min + 20 min core	ER 40 min (spend 15 on form)	5 min of form exercises + ER 45-55 min + 10 min core	Rest	LR 10 miles (in mile 8 do 7 strides, 30 sec each)	Rest
8	ER 40 min	X-train 30 min + 20 min core	ER 35 min (spend 10 on form)	ER 45 min + 10 min core	Rest	LR 7 miles	Rest

Week	Workout 1	Workout 2	Workout 3	Workout 4	Workout 5	Workout 6	Workout 7
9	ER 50-60 min OR Easy Pace 10 + Race Pace 30 + Easy Pace 10	X-train 30 min + 20 min core	ER 35 min (spend 10 on form)	3 min of form exercises + ER 45-55 min +10 min core	Rest	LR 10 miles (in mile 8, do 7 strides, 30 sec each)	Rest
10	ER 50-60 min OR Easy Pace 10 + Race Pace 30 + Easy Pace 10	X-train 30 min + 20 min core	ER 35 min (spend 10 on form)	3 min of form exercises + ER 45-55 min + 10 min core	Rest	LR 10 miles (in miles 5-9, run at race pace)	Rest
11	ER 50-60 min OR Easy Pace 10 + Race Pace 30 + Easy Pace 10	X-train 30 min + 20 min core	ER 35 min (spend 10 on form)	ER 45-55 min + 10 min core	Rest	LR 8 miles (in miles 5-6, run at race pace)	Rest
12 (taper)	ER 50-60 min OR Easy Pace 10 + Race Pace 30 + Easy Pace 10	Rest OR Walk 30 min	ER 35 min OR easy pace 10 + race pace 15 + easy pace 10	Rest	Rest	RACE 13.1!	Rest
13 (recovery)	Rest	Easy walk/run 30 min	Rest	Easy walk/run 30 min OR X-train 30 min	Rest	LR 4 miles + 20 min core	Rest
14 (recovery)	ER 35 min	X-train 30 min + 20 min core	ER 35 min	ER 35 min + 20 min core	Rest	LR 5 miles	Rest

Run/Walk Workout Schedule

Run/walk programs are a terrific way to train for any race distance! Instead of running for the entire training time or distance, a run/walk program incorporates set walk breaks in the training. The walk breaks allow running muscles to rest, your heart rate to recover, and they can help prevent injury—especially for those who are prone to overtraining.

The key is finding a run/walk ratio that works for you. One popular run/walk ratio is 4:1, or four minutes of running, followed by one minute of walking. Another is 10:1 (ten minutes of running, followed by one minute of walking). I once had two participants struggle on every run over four miles, so they transitioned to a 4:1 run/walk program. They immediately found success. In fact, one lady was able to complete an hour and a half training session, simply by allowing for walk breaks every four minutes.

Decide which ratio suits you best. As running becomes easier, do not hesitate to lengthen your running time. You may also decide to use the run/walk ratio only on long runs, and strictly run when covering shorter distances. Do what suits your body best and brings success!

It's best to keep a steady ratio, rather than taking random walk breaks. In other words, stick to your ratio even if you feel you can run an extra thirty seconds. If your four minutes is up, take your walk break. (You can always change your run ratio during your next training run to see if you are ready to lengthen your running time.) A stop watch will help you stay on track. Follow the weekly training logs as written in this book, but instead of running the entire time, substitute your run/walk ratio for the same time or mileage listed for that day's training. Make sure you still spend time warming up and cooling down.

Some walking tips:

- Your walk breaks should be a fast walk. The goal is to lower your heart rate a little and give your running muscles a break *without losing your momentum.*

- Try not to lose too much time in transition between walking and running. It should be a seamless transition. Your form should not change much between the two.

- Keep your arms bent, in running form. Pump your arms, and allow them to help propel you forward.

- Take smaller steps and keep your legs and hips underneath your body. Allow your hips to move and propel you forward. Rather than moving them from side to side, think of them moving in a figure eight. This may feel funny at first!

- Concentrate on forward motion. Up and down movement (that you get when taking big steps) wastes energy.

- Your run/walk cadence will be lower than your run cadence, but still aim for about 160 steps per minute.

- Remember, the goal is to finish, regardless of time. For many people, a run/walk program helps them achieve their goals! (And just because you are running and walking does not automatically make you slower. I have been passed many a time in races by someone using a run/walk program.)

Appendix G — 10K Workout Schedule

WR = Walk/Run, X-train = Cross Train, LW = Long Walk/Run (walk as needed, run when possible)

Week	Workout 1	Workout 2	Workout 3	Workout 4	Workout 5	Workout 6	Workout 7
1	WR 25 min	WR 30 min	X-train 30 min	WR 25 min	Rest	LW 2 miles	Rest
2	WR 30 min	WR 35 min	X-train 30 min	WR 30 min	Rest	LW 3 miles	Rest
3	WR 30 min	WR 35 min	X-train 30 min	WR 30 min	Rest	LW 3 miles	Rest
4	WR 25 min	WR 30 min	X-train 30 min	WR 25 min	Rest	LW 5 miles	Rest
5	WR 35 min	WR 40 min	X-train 30 min	WR 35 min	Rest	LW 3 miles	Rest
6	WR 35 min	WR 40 min	X-train 30 min	WR 35 min	Rest	LW 4 miles	Rest
7	WR 40 min	WR 45 min	X-train 30 min	WR 35 min	Rest	LW 4 miles	Rest
8	WR 35 min	WR 40 min	X-train 30 min	WR 30 min	Rest	LW 3 miles	Rest
9	WR 45 min	WR 35 min	X-train 30 min	WR 40 min	Rest	LW 5 miles	Rest
10	WR 50 min	WR 40 min	X-train 30 min	WR 45 min	Rest	LW 5.5 miles	Rest
11	WR 45 min	WR 30 min	X-train 30 min	WR 40 min	Rest	LW 4 miles	Rest
12	WR 40 min	Race pace 20 min	WR 30 min	Rest	Rest	Race 6.2!!	Rest

Notes

Week 1 – God's Training Plan

1 Ortberg, John. *The Life You've Always Wanted*. (2002). Grand Rapids: Zondervan, pp. 42-43.

2 Moore, Beth. *Breaking Free*, video session 8. (2009). Nashville: Lifeway Christian Resources.

3 Noakes, Timothy. *Lore of Running*. (2002). Champaign, IL: Human Kinetics, p. 289.

Week 2 – Building the Foundation Through Core Training

1 Noakes, p. 278.

2 Noakes, p. 311.

3 Ibid.

4 Johnson, Kelly. *Why building a base in marathon training is key*. OregonLive.com. blog.oregonlive.com/runoregon/2009/02/building_a_base_in_marathon_tr.html.

5 Ibid.

6 Sports Fitness Advisor. www.sport-fitness-advisor.com/endurancetraining.html.

7 Running Online. *Calculate Your Heart Rate Zones*. www.runningonline.com/zine/Health/148.sht.

8 Ibid.

9 Blue Letter Bible. www.blueletterbible.org/lang/lexicon/lexicon.cfm?strongs=G2310.

10 National Academy of Sports Medicine. (2007). *NASM Essentials of Personal Fitness Training*. Philadelphia, PA: Lippincott, Williams & Wilkins. Pp.

287

198-199.

11 The Nelson Study Bible. New King James Version. (1997). Page 161. Nashville, TN: Thomas Nelson.

Week 3 – Moving Forward in Faith

1 Blue Letter Bible. www.blueletterbible.org/lang/lexicon/lexicon. cfm?Strongs=G4102.

2 Moore, Beth. (2008). *Believing God*. Nashville, TN: LifeWay Press. Pages 18-19.

3 Blue Letter Bible. www.blueletterbible.org/lang/lexicon/lexicon. cfm?Strongs=G4043.

4 See Genesis 12:11-13 and Genesis 20:1-2.

Week 4 – Our Bodies as Temples

1 Holt, David. "Atltitude Training, Running, and Racing." Running Dialog. home.sprynet.com/~holtrun/altitude.htm.

2 Alcorn, Randy. *Heaven*. (2004). Carol Stream, IL: Tyndale House Publishers. Page 57.

3 McNutt, Matthew. "The Spirituality of Physical Health." Youth Specialties. www.youthspecialties.com/articles/the-spirituality-of-physical-health.

4 Shirer, Priscilla, & Moore, Beth. *Anointed, Transformed, Redeemed: A Study of David*. (2008). Nashville, TN: Lifeway Christian Resources. Page 17.

5 Fields, Leslie Leyland. (2010, November). "A Feast Fit for a King." Christianity Today. www.christianitytoday.com/ct/2010/november/9.22. html?start=6.

6 Centers for Disease Control and Prevention. "FASTATS: Overweight Prevalence." www.cdc.gov/nchs/fastats/overwt.htm.

7 Bevere, Lisa. *You are Not What You Weigh*. (2006). Lake Mary: Siloam

Press. Page 3.

8 Bevere. Page 92.

9 Bratman, Steven. "Health Food Junkie." Beyond Vegetarianism. www.beyondveg.com/bratman-s/hfj/hf-junkie-1a.shtml.

10 Bevere, Page 33.

11 Casey, John. "The Hidden Ingredients that can Sabotage Your Diet." MedicineNet. www.medicinenet.com/script/main/art.asp?articlekey=56589.

12 "Association recommends Americans cut intake of added sugars." American Heart Association. www.newsroom.heart.org/index.php?s=43&item=800.

13 National Academy of Sports Medicine. *NASM Essentials of Personal Fitness Training.* (2008). Philadelphia: Lippincott, Williams, and Wilkins. Page 183.

14 Clark, Nancy. *Nancy Clark's Sports Nutrition Guidebook.* (2008). Human Kinetics. Page 149.

15 Clark. Page 151.

16 Clark. Page 152.

17 Clark. Page 156.

Week 5 – Proper Form

1 Wallack, Roy. *Run For Life.* (2009). New York: Skyhorse Publishing. Page 13.

2 Ibid.

3 Wallack, page 22.

4 Wallack, page 17.

5 "Improve Your Running with Proper Breathing." Articlesbase. http://www.articlesbase.com/sports-and-fitness-articles/improve-your-running-with-proper-breathing-45455.html.

6 Blue Letter Bible. "Dictionary and Word Search for shalowm (Strong's 7965)." December 27, 2010. http://www.blueletterbible.org/lang/lexicon/lexicon.cfm?strongs=H7965&t=KJV&page=9.

7 Moore, Beth. *Breaking Free*. (2009). Nashville: Lifeway Press. Page 224.

8 National Academy of Sports Medicine. *NASM Essentials of Personal Fitness Training*. (2008). Philadelphia: Lippincott, Williams and Wilkins. Pages 143-144.

9 "Posture Problems." Ask The Trainer. (2008). http://askthetrainer.com/posture-problems.html.

Week 6 – Matters of the Heart

1 National Academy of Sports Medicine. *NASM Essentials of Personal Fitness Training*. (2008). Philadelphia: Lippincott, Williams and Wilkins. Page 40.

2 De Nies, Yunji. "Just How Bad are 'America's Unhealthiest Meals'?" ABC News. http://abcnews.go.com/WN/Health/story?id=8013761&page=1.

3 "Heart disease." MedlinePlus Medical Encyclopedia. http://www.nlm.nih.gov/medlineplus/ency/article/000147.htm.

4 Pallarito, Karen. "Diet and Fitness: A Proven Path for Heart Health." ABC News HealthDay. http://abcnews.go.com/Health/Healthday/story?id=4508172&page=1.

5 Blue Letter Bible. "Dictionary and Word Search for *leb* (Strong's 3820)." http://www.blueletterbible.org/lang/lexicon/lexicon.cfm?Strongs=H3820&t=KJV.

6 Blue Letter Bible. "Dictionary and Word Search for *kardia* (Strong's 2588)." http:// www.blueletterbible.org/lang/lexicon/lexicon.cfm?strongs=G2588.

7 Editorial staff. "God's Quiet Signature." Christianity Today. December 2010. Page 57.

8 Blue Letter Bible. "Dictionary and Word Search for *natsar* (Strong's 5341)." http:// www.blueletterbible.org/lang/lexicon/lexicon.cfm?strongs=H5341&t=KJV.

9 Warren, Kay. *Dangerous Surrender*. (2007). Grand Rapids: Zondervan. Page 128.

Week 7– Hitting the Wall

1 Latta, Sara. "Hitting 'The Wall.'" Marathon & Beyond. 2003. http://www.marathonandbeyond.com/choices/latta.htm.

2 Shea, Sarah Bowen. "Carbs on the Run." Runner's World. August, 2008. http://www.runnersworld.com/article/1,7124,s6-242-301--12826-0,00.html.

3 Noakes, Timothy. *The Lore of Running* (3rd ed.). (2001). Champaign, IL: Human Kinetics. Page 148.

4 Latta.

5 Pierce, Bill, Murr, Scott, & Moss, Ray. *Run Less, Run Faster.* (2007). Emmaus, PA: Rodale Books. Page 26.

6 Ibid.

7 Pierce, page 17.

8 Pierce, page 27.

9 Noakes, page 594.

10 Noakes, page 260.

11 Noakes, p. 260,594

12 Ortberg, John. *The Life You've Always Wanted.* (2002). Grand Rapids: Zondervan. Page 52.

13 Overcome. Dictionary.com. http://dictionary.reference.com/browse/overcome.

Week 8 – Rest and Relaxation

1 Eyestone, Ed. "The Rest is Easy." Runners World. http://www.runnersworld.com/article/0,7120,s6-238-267--13104-0,00.html.

2 Karnazes, Dean. *50/50.* (2008). New York: Wellness Central. Page 51.

3 Bowen Shea, Sarah. "Chasing Zzzzs." Runners World. http://www.runnersworld.com/article/0,7120,s6-238-267--8028-2-1-2,00.html.

4 Karnazes, page 51.

5 Mann, Denise. "Sleep and Weight Gain." WebMD. http://www.webmd. com/sleep-disorders/excessive-sleepiness-10/lack-of-sleep-weight-gain.

6 Blue Letter Bible. "Dictionary and Word Search for *shabath* (Strong's 7673)". 27 Dec 2010. http://www.blueletterbible.org/lang/lexicon/Lexicon. cfm?Strongs=H7673&t=KJV.

7 "Refresh." Dictionary.com. http://dictionary.reference.com/browse/ refresh.

8 Ortberg, John. *The Life You've Always Wanted*. (2002). Grand Rapids: Zondervan. Page 63.

9 Ortberg, page 70.

10 Ortberg, page 86.

Week 9 – Cognitive Restructuring

1 Barcott, Bruce. (2010). "Kara Goucher's Mind Gains." Runner's World. http://www.runnersworld.com/article/1,7120,s6-243-297--13431-0,00.html.

2 Noakes, Timothy. *The Lore of Running* (3rd ed.). (2001). Champaign, IL: Human Kinetics. Page 625.

3 Noakes, page 520.

4 Scott, Dagney. *Runner's World Complete Book of Women's Running*. (2000). Emmaus, PA: Rodale Press. Page 151.

5 "Cognitive restructuring." Reference.com. http://www.reference.com/ browse/cognitive+restructuring.

6 Douban, Gigi. (2007). "Choice Words." (2007). http://www.runnersworld. com/article/0,7120,s6-238-267--11776-2-2-2,00.html.

7 Ibid.

8 Ibid.

9 Brant, John. (2007). "A Mile For Your Thoughts." Runner's World. http:// www.runnersworld.com/article/1,7124,s6-238-520--11824-0,00.html.

10 Backus, William. The Healing Power of a Christian Mind. (1996). Grand

Rapids: Baker Publishing Group. Page 117.

11 Backus, p.115.

12 Backus, p 116.

13 Backus, p 117.

14 *"Reject* Synonyms, *Reject* Antonyms." Thesaurus.com. http://thesaurus. com/browse/reject.

15 Ibid.

16 *"Control* Synonyms, *Control* Antonyms." Thesaurus.com. http://thesaurus. com/browse/control.

17 Ibid.

18 Backus, p.117.

Week 10 – Building Up and Tearing Down

1 Green, Daniel J. and Ekeroth, Christine J. (editors). *Ace's Group Fitness Instructor Manual: A Guide for Fitness Professionals,* second edition. (2007). Knoxville: Power System. Page 13.

2 Wilmore, Jack, Costill, David L., and Kenney, W. Larry. *Physiology of Sport and Exercise.* (2008). Champaign, IL: Human Kinetics. Page 310.

3 *Life Application Study Bible NLT.* (1996). Carol Stream, IL: Tyndale House Publishers.

4 "Loan." Dictionary.com. http://dictionary.reference.com/browse/loan.

5 Spurgeon, Charles Haddon. "Blessing for Blessing." http://www.bluelet-terbible.org/commentaries/comm_view.cfm?AuthorID=10&contentID= 3877&commInfo=16&topic=Sermons& ar=Eph_1_3.

6 Clark, Michael A., Lucett, Scott, Corn, Rodney J. *NASM Essentials of Personal Fitness Training Third Edition.* (2008). Philadelphia, PA: Lippincott, Williams & Wilkins. Page 273.

7 Finke, Patti and Warren. *Marathoning, Start to Finish,* 4th edition. (2001). Tualitin, OR: wY'east Consulting. Page 15.

8 Scott, Dagney. *Runner's World Complete Book of Women's Running.* (2000). Emmaus, PA: Rodale Publishing. Page 55.

9 Life Application Study Bible NLT, page 1966.

10 Smith, Chuck. "John 15." Blue Letter Bible. (2005.) http:// www.blueletterbible.org/commentaries/comm_view.cfm?AuthorID=1&contentID=7163&commInfo=25&topic=John.

11 Mroczek, Christy. "How to Prune Grapes: Grape Vineyard Care for Winter." (2008). http://www.suite101.com/content/how-to-prune-grapes-a60937.

12 "Pruning." Britannica Online Encyclopedia. (2011.) http://www.britannica.com/EBchecked/topic/480857/pruning.

Week 11 – Race Community

1 "Statistics." Running USA. http://www.runningusa.org/statistics.

2 Armstrong, Kristin. *Strength for the Climb.* (2007). Boston: Hachette Book Group. Page 239.

3 Jill Geer. "USATF Amends Headphone Rule." USA Track & Field. 12-22-2008. http://www.usatf.org/news/view.aspx?DUID=USATF_2008_12_22_10_22_16.

Week 12 – Final Preparations

1 Jhung, Lisa. "Is Your Taper Too Long?" Runner's World. September 19, 2007. http://www.runnersworld.com/article/0,7120,s6-238-244--12123-2-1-2,00.html.

2 The Iliotibial (IT) Band is a group of fibers along the outside of the thigh that can cause pain on the outside of runners' knees. You can read more about this in Appendix D where I talk about signs of injury, what they mean, and how to prevent them.

3 Newsboys. *Stay Strong. The Ultimate Collection.* 2007, Sparrow Records.

Running by The Book Communities

Christian running coach Corinne Baur is passionate about helping churches and groups create faith-based running programs. To help group leaders, Corinne has compiled a RBTB Leader's guide, offering chapter by chapter suggestions, tips and solutions for leading a successful Running by The Book group, available for free at RunningByTheBook.com.

Visit her Facebook site at facebook.com/RunningByTheBook where you can join her online community for tips, encouragement and meet others on their "race."

If you are interested in having Corinne speak to your group, please contact her at: info@runningbythebook.com.